THE GRANNY SQUARE CROCHET BIBLE

THE GRANNY SQUARE CROCHET BIBLE

Lynne Rowe

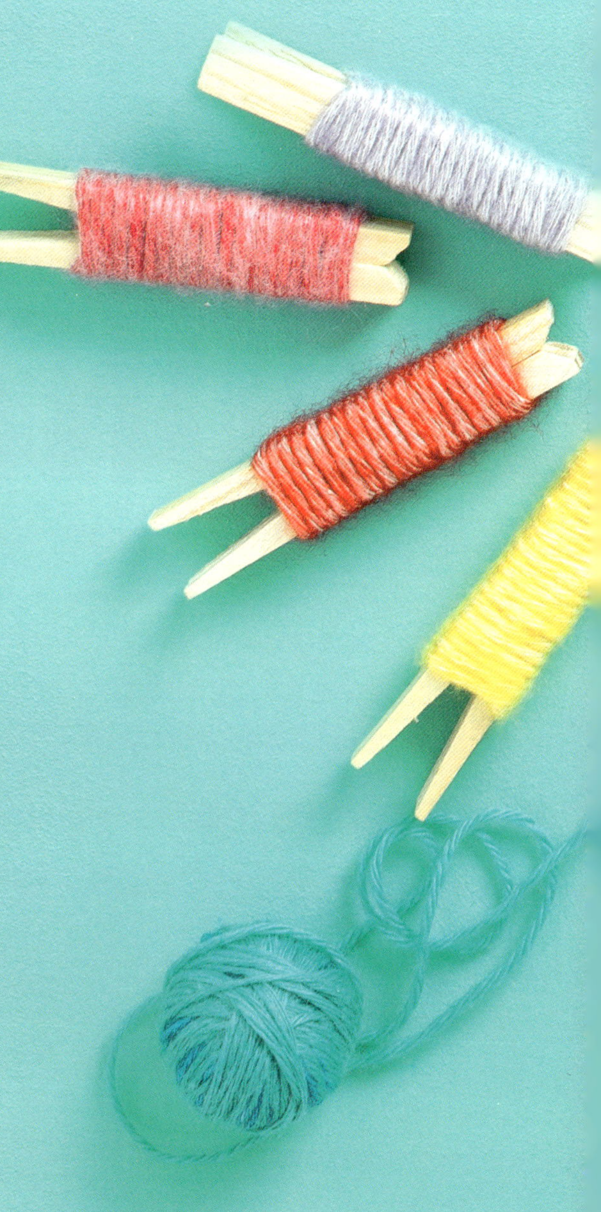

Everything you need to know about how to crochet granny squares

DAVID & CHARLES
— PUBLISHING —

www.davidandcharles.com

CONTENTS

INTRODUCTION

There is so much I love about crochet, from working simple, repetitive, and calming stitches, to creating colorful projects that brighten up my day. But one of my absolute favorite things to crochet is the classic granny square.

I don't know of another technique that is so versatile. You have the freedom to choose whether you keep it simple and work using a single color, or go bold and use all the colors of the rainbow for a multi-colored masterpiece. You can even try a monochrome look by crocheting in black and white. The possibilities are endless, and the choice is in the hands of the maker, giving us the perfect opportunity to be as creative and colorful as we like.

The adaptability and simplicity of granny squares makes them a firm favorite among crocheters of all skill levels. Granny squares are a great project for a beginner, because you only need to learn one main stitch for a classic granny square. You can practice by making lots of different squares, which you can then join together to make something beautiful and useful. This modular nature allows for easy construction of larger projects, making them an ideal choice for everything from blankets and scarves to bags and clothing.

Granny squares are now at the height of fashion, and if you're eager to join the granny square trend, then you're in the right place. With my step-by-step tutorials, I will ease you into the never-ending world of granny squares. By taking small steps, and getting comfortable with terms and techniques, you'll soon master the art of the humble granny square. In no time at all you'll be moving on to more intricate motifs.

Get ready to let your imagination and creativity run wild as you start creating your own handmade clothes and accessories, and most of all, have lots of fun.

Cheers to the timeless granny square.

Lynne x

HOW TO USE THIS BOOK

If you are completely new to granny squares crochet, then this is the perfect place to begin. This book will guide you step-by-step through the world of crocheting granny square motifs, from understanding the basics, to selecting your yarn and hook ready to start your journey.

For those of you who are already familiar with granny square fundamentals, this book offers a variety of new motifs to explore, ranging from different shapes and designs, to joining options and decorative edgings. In no time at all your granny square knowledge will have you hooking up squares in all shapes, sizes, and colors.

To help you practice, and become really confident with granny square crochet, there are also lots of gorgeous, fun projects to create, from creative homewares and colorful blankets to a stylish cardigan and a cozy cowl. Whether you want to start with a quick make or something more substantial, you'll find lots of choice for everyone in this colorful array of patterns.

Once you have mastered the basics you can try all the different motifs, then choose your first project and put your new-found knowledge and skills to the test.

If at any point you get stuck, you can flick through the book and use it as a trusty reference guide.

HERE IS YOUR ROADMAP TO FOLLOW, BEFORE YOU START CROCHETING YOUR FIRST MOTIF

TOOLS AND MATERIALS

Begin by reading the Tools and Materials section to make informed choices about yarn and hook selection.

STITCH NAMES

Note that all the patterns are written using US crochet terms. See Techniques: US/UK Conversions for a conversion table.

ALL ABOUT GRANNY SQUARES

Dive into the Granny Square Anatomy section to grasp the essentials of creating a classic granny square.

PRACTICE THE GRANNY SQUARE STITCH

Familiarize yourself with the granny square stitch on a flat crochet piece, to get comfortable with its rhythm and feel.

ALL ABOUT SIZE

Explore how different yarn and hook sizes impact the final dimensions of your motif in the All About Size section.

CHARTS

Explore the Charts section and compare the chart to your stitches to understand how it corresponds to the stitches being made.

CROCHET STITCHES AND TECHNIQUES

If necessary, brush up on your general crochet stitch knowledge with the help of illustrated instructions in the Techniques section.

TOOLS AND MATERIALS

The best thing about crocheting granny squares is that you only need a few different materials. All you need to get started is a hook, yarn, tapestry needle, and scissors. Whether you're looking to make small projects like bags, or larger-scale projects like blankets or garments, granny square projects offer endless possibilities with minimal investment. As with other projects, there are lots of extra tools and materials you can invest in, so I've written a handy guide to help you choose from the different products available.

HOOKS

This book uses a variety of hook sizes for different motifs and projects. The required hook size will depend on the yarn thickness and will be listed at the beginning of each pattern. Most projects will use the hook size recommended on the yarn label.

Hooks come in different materials, including wood, bamboo, metal, and composite, and some hooks combine materials, like a wooden handle with a metal hook. Ergonomic hooks are also available; they are designed for a comfortable grip to help reduce strain injuries. The main thing is to try different hooks, to help you determine which you prefer to crochet with. If you feel comfortable with your hook, you are more likely to achieve neat crochet stitches and to enjoy the process of making.

YARN

For practicing with the motifs, you can use any yarn thickness you have on hand, along with the recommended hook size for that yarn. This allows you to practice without the need for buying any extra yarn. Each motif pattern gives the yarn thickness and the number of colors you'll need.

For the projects themselves, the specific yarn is listed at the start of each pattern, along with the quantities required and key details like thickness and length (in yards or meters) per ball. You can use a different brand of yarn if you prefer, but make sure that it is the same thickness and that the length (yardage/meterage) of each ball is at least the same (or greater), otherwise you may run out of yarn.

Scheepjes
METROPOLIS

TAPESTRY/YARN NEEDLE

You will need a large-eyed tapestry/yarn needle for weaving in ends. A blunt-ended needle is recommended because a sharp needle will split your yarn and spoil your stitches.

SCISSORS

Keep a small pair of sharp scissors handy for snipping yarn after weaving in your ends. If your scissors are particularly pointy, a protective cover is recommended, both for personal safety and also to protect the other things in your project bag, including your projects. Don't be tempted to try and snap yarn with your fingers, as this can distort your work and also hurt your hands.

REMOVABLE OR LOCKING STITCH MARKERS

These are usually made of plastic or metal and open and close like a safety pin. They are mainly used in this book to hold pieces together before you join them, so it is essential that you use stitch markers that can be removed easily. You can lay motifs side-by-side and "pin" them together with your stitch markers before you start to join them with crochet or sewing. It is possible to use safety pins instead, but these can split your yarn and damage stitches.

TAPE MEASURE

The size and finished measurements of motifs and projects are provided, so you will need a tape measure to check the measurements of your own motifs and projects. You will also need to measure your swatches to make sure that you are achieving the same gauge (tension). I would recommend a retractable tape measure so that it doesn't become tangled up with other items in your project bag.

NOTEBOOK AND PEN OR PENCIL

I tend to consider a notebook and pen or pencil as an essential part of my toolkit, because it's really handy to be able to note down any changes that you make to a pattern, so that you remember them for next time.

PROJECT BAG

Canvas totes, or handmade project bags, are perfect for keeping everything together, and you can choose the size to suit your project. You don't need to buy anything expensive; a re-usable shopping tote will be perfect.

BLOCKING BOARDS

Blocking mats can be used individually for small motifs and small projects or slotted together to create larger mats for larger projects. They are usually made from colored foam and come in packs of six or nine blocks that can be joined together to make a strip or one larger block.

RUST-PROOF PINS

These are vital for blocking your work. Use pins with colored heads so that they are visible and don't get lost in your crochet.

SPRAY WATER BOTTLE

A small bottle for water is perfect to help wet your pieces for blocking.

STEAMER

Using a handheld steamer for crochet is a great way to block your finished pieces quickly and effectively. The steam helps to relax the fibers, allowing you to shape your crochet projects without fully soaking them. Simply hold the steamer a few inches away from the fabric, gently applying steam while shaping the piece with your hands.

ALL ABOUT GRANNY SQUARES

Crocheting a classic granny square is a great way to use up oddments of yarn, and some of the most amazing granny square blankets feature a fabulous array of color, and really stand out as being unique. I doubt that you will ever get bored with the classic granny square, because it is so versatile, as well as soothing to stitch. By the end of this chapter, you'll be ready to hook up your first granny square with confidence.

THE BENEFITS OF THE GRANNY

- **Repetition and mindfulness:** The repetition of the double crochet stitch provides a calming rhythm that is hard to beat, and when it's worked in groups of 3dc in the granny stitch, it provides a powerful tool for mindfulness. You'll soon find that you always need a granny square blanket on the go, so that you can turn to it every day for a few moments to help you relax and unwind.
- **Using your stash:** The best thing about this versatile motif is that you can raid your yarn stash to practice, and before you know it, you'll have a stack of classic granny squares, ready to join together to create a larger project.
- **Learning crochet skills:** As well as being fun and adaptable, granny squares provide a fantastic foundation for learning various crochet skills that will become the cornerstone of your crochet journey. In this chapter we explore everything you need to know to get started, from understanding the basic structure of a granny square, to learning the basic granny stitch and reading charts. You'll learn all about gauge (tension) and how to measure a square so that you can check if you are working to the right size, and you'll learn how different yarns and hook sizes can affect the size of your square.

GRANNY SQUARE ANATOMY

In this section, we'll break down the key components of a classic crochet granny square. Each part of the granny square has a specific function and contributes to the overall structure and appearance. By understanding the anatomy of a granny square, you'll be better equipped to follow patterns, troubleshoot issues, and even design your own squares. We'll explore these parts in detail to help you create beautiful and consistent granny squares.

CENTER RING

This is the starting point of the granny square. It is a small ring, either created by a series of chain stitches that are joined with a slip stitch to form a ring, or it can be made with a more advanced technique called a magic ring or an adjustable ring. The first round of the granny square motif is worked into the center of this ring.

ROUNDS

Granny squares are built up by working in rounds. The first round is worked in the center ring, then each subsequent round is worked into the spaces between groups of stitches.

CLUSTERS OR DC-GROUPS

The basic building block of a granny square is the cluster, which is a group of three double crochet stitches that are worked into the same space or stitch. These clusters are often called groups or dc-groups. In this book we use the term dc-groups.

BEGINNING CHAINS

Each time you start a round, you begin with three chain stitches, instead of a double crochet. These chain stitches bring your hook to the correct height to work the next double crochet stitch, and they count as a double crochet stitch.

CHAIN SPACES

Between clusters or dc-groups, chain stitches can be used to create spaces. These spaces give the granny square its characteristic open and airy look. The corner spaces usually have more chain stitches to help shape the motif. Along the sides there is usually one chain stitch in between the dc-groups. However, if a more closed appearance is required, there are no chain stitches between the side dc-groups.

CORNERS

The corners of a granny square are formed by working multiple dc-groups into the same space, usually separated by chain stitches. This increases the square's size evenly. For example, the classic granny square has two lots of 3dc-groups in each corner, which are separated by two chain stitches.

SIDES

The sides of the square are made up of a series of 3dc-groups, worked into the chain spaces from the previous round.

SLIP STITCHES

These are used to join rounds or move the working yarn along the stitches to the correct position for the next round.

CENTER RING
SLIP STITCHES
BEGINNING CHAINS
ROUND
SIDE
CHAIN SPACE
CORNER
CLUSTER OR 3DC-GROUP

THE GRANNY SQUARE STITCH

The granny stitch is the fundamental crochet technique that forms the iconic granny square pattern. To help you understand and practice this stitch, we'll start by working it in rows instead of rounds. This simplifies the process and helps you get comfortable with the basic components, and it's a great opportunity to try out the stitch before you start your granny square motifs.

STARTING CHAIN

Begin with a slip knot on your hook. Chain a multiple of 3, plus 4 additional ch. For example, ch18 (which is a multiple of 3) plus 4 additional ch—so ch22 in total.

FIRST ROW (RIGHT SIDE)

1. 1dc in fourth chain from hook (the skipped 3 ch are your beginning ch-3, and also count as your first dc). You have created your edge stitches **(A)**.

2. *Skip next 2 ch, work 3dc in next ch*; rep from * to * across the row, to last 3 sts. You have created your 3dc-groups for the granny stitch.

3. Skip next 2 ch, work 2dc in last chain. You have created your edge stitches **(B)**. From your original 22 ch, you now have 19 sts. Turn your work.

MATERIALS NEEDED

Yarn of your choice

Crochet hook size recommended for your yarn

Scissors

Yarn needle (for weaving in ends)

BASIC STITCHES TO KNOW

- **Chain (ch):** The foundation stitch for working in rows. Also used to begin each row.
- **Double crochet (dc):** A tall stitch that makes up the granny stitch. In UK terms this double crochet is called treble crochet (tr).

TIPS FOR PRACTICING

- **Consistency:** Keep your gauge (tension) even for a uniform appearance.
- **Counting:** Regularly count your stitches to ensure accuracy.
- **Further experimentation:** If you want to create a more open stitch, you can add a chain (ch1) between the clusters in each row. This will give your work a lighter and looser feel and is similar to the Classic Granny Squares in Getting Started. Feel free to experiment with both styles (with and without the ch1), to find the one you like best!

SECOND ROW (WRONG SIDE)

4. Ch3 (counts as first dc), skip next dc, work 3dc in the space between 3dc-groups of the previous row **(C)**.

5. Continue working 3dc in each space between dc-groups across the row. At the end of the row, dc in the top ch of the beginning ch-3 from the previous row **(D)**. You now have 20 sts. Turn your work.

THIRD ROW (RIGHT SIDE)

6. Ch3 (counts as first dc), work 1dc in same stitch at base of beginning ch-3. You have created your edge stitches **(E)**. *Skip next 3dc-group, work 3dc in next space between 3dc-groups*; repeat from * to * across the row, to last dc. You have created your 3dc-groups for your granny stitch.

7. Work 2dc in this last st. You have created your edge stitches. You now have 19 stitches. Turn your work.

NOTE: *The second and third rows form the granny stitch pattern.*

SUBSEQUENT ROWS

Repeat the second and third rows, as many times as desired **(F)**, noting that on Row 2 you will have 1 stitch more than on Row 3, which is correct for this stitch pattern.

FASTENING OFF

When you have reached your desired length, cut the yarn, place the yarn over the hook and pull it through the final stitch. Pull tight to form a knot. Weave your end into the wrong side of your work and through the base of the double crochet stitches (see Techniques: Weaving in Ends). Snip the yarn close to the stitches.

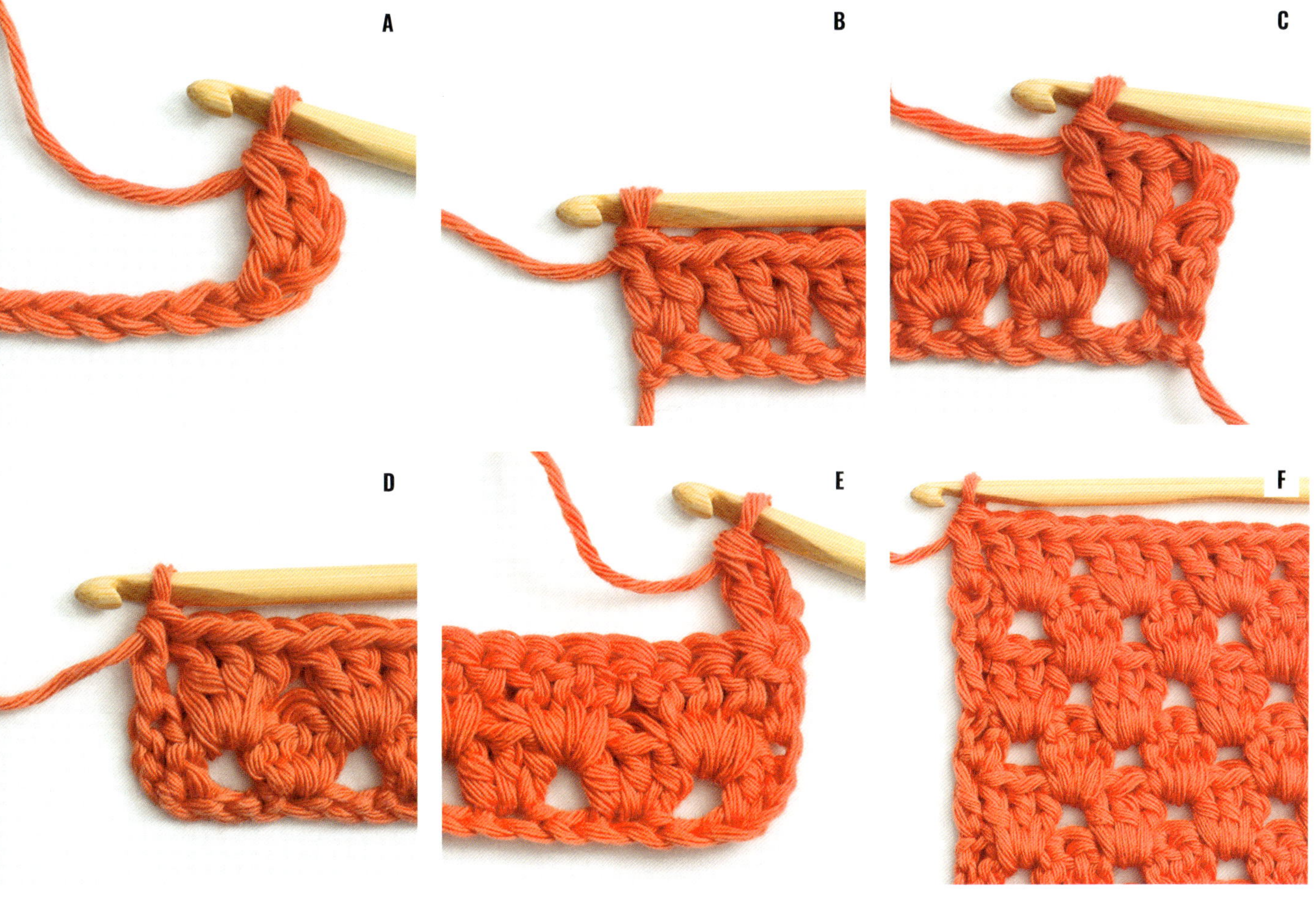

ALL ABOUT SIZE

The size of your granny square can vary significantly depending on the yarn and hook you use, and the number of rounds that you work. The thickness of the yarn, known as the yarn weight, and the size of your crochet hook, both play crucial roles in determining the final dimensions of your granny square.

YARN THICKNESS

Yarn weight ranges from very fine (lace weight) to very thick (super bulky). Lighter weight yarns, such as lace weight or fingering weight (4ply), will produce much smaller and more delicate granny squares. In contrast, using a heavier yarn like bulky (chunky) or super bulky (super chunky) will result in larger and more substantial squares. The choice of yarn weight should match the intended use of your project, whether it's for a delicate doily or a warm, cozy blanket.

HOOK SIZE

The crochet hook size also influences the size of your granny square. A larger hook creates bigger stitches, resulting in a larger square. Conversely, a smaller hook produces tighter stitches, making the square smaller. It's important to match the hook size with the yarn thickness to maintain the proper gauge (tension) and drape. Most yarn labels suggest an appropriate hook size, but experimenting with different sizes can help you achieve the exact dimensions you want.

GAUGE (TENSION)

Finally, your personal gauge also affects the size. If you crochet tightly, your squares may be smaller, and if you crochet loosely, they may be larger. Practicing with different hooks and yarns, and making swatches, can help you find the right combination for your project. You can read more about achieving size in the next section, which covers all about gauge.

DIFFERENCE IN SIZE BETWEEN SQUARES

Here is a guide to the recommended hook size for different yarn thicknesses. The yarn and hook size you choose will determine the height of the double crochet stitches in your square. The thicker your yarn and the larger your hook, the taller your double crochet stitches will be.

- Lace weight using US B/1 (2mm) hook **(A)**.
- Fingering (4ply) using US C/2 or D/3 (3mm) hook **(B)**.
- Light worsted (double knitting) using US G/6 (4mm) hook **(C)**.
- Worsted (aran weight) using US 7 or US H/8 (4.5mm or 5mm) hook **(D)**.
- Bulky (chunky) using US J/10, K10½ or L11 (6mm, 7mm, or 8mm) hook **(E)**.
- Super bulky (super chunky) using US M/N13, N/P 15, or O (9mm, 10mm, or 12mm) hook **(F)**.

C
A
B
D
F
E

GAUGE

Gauge (or tension) refers to how tightly or loosely you crochet, and it directly impacts the finished size and shape of your granny squares. Consistent gauge ensures that all your squares are uniform in size, making assembly easier and resulting in a polished, professional-looking finished product.

Achieving and maintaining the correct gauge when crocheting granny squares is essential for several reasons.

- Firstly, when joining multiple squares of the same size together, it is important that all squares match the specific dimensions in the pattern so that you can join them neatly. If your squares are inconsistent in size due to varying gauge, you may struggle to align and join them properly, leading to a distorted or uneven project.
- Secondly, maintaining consistent gauge also ensures that your granny squares have a uniform drape and feel. Even for decorative items like blankets or pillows, uniform gauge ensures that the fabric lies flat and looks neat.
- Thirdly, achieving the correct gauge for garments is especially important to ensure the garment fits properly, drapes as intended, and is comfortable to wear.

Regularly checking your gauge as you work, and making adjustments as needed, can help you create projects that are the correct size, as well as looking well-made.

CHECKING YOUR GAUGE

Start by making a gauge swatch. This is a small sample square worked in the same yarn and hook size you plan to use for your project. If you are following a pattern, this information will be included at the beginning of the pattern.

Measure your swatch to see if it matches the gauge that is specified in your pattern. For a granny square or a square motif, usually the measurements are given for a specific number of rounds.

FOR EXAMPLE:

Five rounds of granny square motif measure 4 x 4in (10 x 10cm), using a US E/4 (3.5mm) hook and fingering (4ply) weight yarn.

To check your gauge, you would work the motif for 5 rounds, then measure it.

WHAT TO DO IF YOUR GAUGE DOESN'T MATCH

Adjusting your hook size helps you achieve the correct gauge without altering your crocheting style too drastically.

- If your swatch is too small, try again using a hook that is the next size larger.
- If it's too large, try again, using a hook that is the next size smaller.

Regularly checking your gauge as you work, and adjusting it as needed, can help you to create beautiful, professional-quality projects.

CHARTS

Granny square charts are visual representations of the stitches needed to create a granny square. Whilst they can appear off-putting at first, once you become familiar with reading crochet charts you'll see they are an excellent way to see the entire pattern at a glance—and they can be easier to follow than written instructions. They can help you to see where stitches go, and help you decipher long and often complicated written instructions.

KEY ELEMENTS OF A GRANNY SQUARE CHART

Each type of stitch is represented by a specific symbol, with a key usually included with the chart. Some groups of stitches, such as the granny stitch 3dc-group, have their own special symbol, as do starting chains. This means that you can read a chart instead of the written instructions, because everything you need is included. Stitches are also shown relative to size, which also helps visualize how the stitch pattern will look.

CHART OVERVIEW

- Most granny square charts start in the center and work outward in rounds. The center is often marked with a small circle, or a circle of chain stitches.
- Each round of the granny square is represented as a layer of symbols around the center and rounds can be numbered to help you keep track of your progress.
- Charts often have arrows to indicate the direction of stitching. Most granny squares are worked in rounds that are joined.
- Circular charts are read counterclockwise. Charts for patterns worked in rows are usually read from right to left for odd-number (RS) rows and left to right for even-number (WS) rows—unless the pattern states otherwise.

GRANNY SQUARE SYMBOLS INCLUDE

Chain ring: A ring of chain stitches

Magic ring (or center ring): A small circle outline

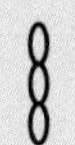
Beginning chain: A series of chain stitches stacked on top of each other to symbolize the beginning of a round. For a classic granny square, this is 3 chains

Chain (ch): A small oval

Slip stitch (slst): A small dot or a filled-in circle

Single crochet (sc): A small cross

Half double crochet (hdc): A vertical line with a short top bar

Double crochet (dc): A vertical line with a slash through the line, and a short top bar

Treble crochet (tr): A vertical line with two slashes through the line, and a short top bar

3dc-group: 3 double crochet stitch symbols in a V-shape to indicate they are worked into one stitch or space

3tr-CL: 3 treble stitches in an upside down V-shape to indicate they are joined at the top

Puff-stitch (puff-st): several double crochet stitches with curved rather than vertical lines and joined at top and bottom

READING THE CHARTS

First look at the chart's key or legend to understand what each symbol means. Familiarize yourself with these symbols before starting work.

Find the starting point: Locate the center of the chart. This is where you will begin your granny square. This is the center ring or loop and is sometimes called the foundation ring.

Round 1: Work your way outward from the center. The beginning of each round is the same, starting with the beginning chain. This is 3 chains stacked on top of each other and is easy to differentiate from the double crochet symbols. From this beginning ch-3, follow the chart counterclockwise, working the symbols in the order presented, and working these stitches into the center ring. When you reach the end of the round, you will see the slip stitch symbol, to indicate that you join the round. You always join the round with a slip stitch into the top of the beginning ch-3. If the next round is shown in a different color, you can now cut your yarn and fasten off your first round.

Subsequent rounds: To join a new color, you can check the chart to locate the beginning ch-3 of the next round, to join the yarn in the correct place. Then you are ready to follow the symbols as before, this time working into the chain spaces made on the previous rounds.

TIPS FOR SUCCESS

- Most diagrams are drawn for right-handed crocheters and you follow the symbols around in a counterclockwise direction, working your crochet from right to left. If you're left-handed, you can read the symbols in the same direction, but you will crochet in a clockwise direction instead, from left to right.
- Sometimes a flat motif worked in the round may ask you to "turn" and work stitches in the other direction, then turn again. This change should be marked on the stitch diagram or specified in the pattern notes.
- Practice with this simple granny square chart to build your confidence.
- If you have both a chart and written instructions, compare the two of them to see how they align.
- By understanding these key elements and steps, you'll be able to read and follow the granny square charts in this book with ease.

GETTING STARTED

The first basic recipe will take you step-by-step through the process of crocheting a classic granny square motif, first using a different color for each round, then by using the same color throughout. Whilst they follow the same basic steps, there are subtle differences at the start of the round, and it's good to get these techniques under your belt from the very beginning of your journey. Full instructions are included, so don't worry about this for now.

BEFORE YOU BEGIN

- **Embrace the simplicity:** Granny squares can be crocheted in numerous different ways, and each designer will have their own preference. This book focuses on the simplest methods to get you started on your crochet journey.
- **Check your gauge/tension:** If specific gauge or motif measurements are provided, make sure your gauge is accurate before starting. This way your motifs will turn out the correct size (see Gauge).
- **Yarn and hook considerations:** Yarn quantities are provided, but these may ultimately vary, based on your chosen yarn thickness and hook size.
- **Brush up your skills:** If you need to refresh your crochet skills and knowledge, refer to the Techniques section for guidance.
- **Embrace mistakes:** Mistakes happen, and that's okay! Crochet allows for easy unraveling of stitches, giving you the chance to try again, and again.

MOTIF 1: MULTI-COLOR CLASSIC GRANNY SQUARE

The classic granny square is often called a traditional granny square, and can often be referred to as a motif, rather than a square. But they all mean the same thing, and these terms are used interchangeably.

CLASSIC GRANNY SQUARE FACTS

- This traditional square is made by working groups of 3dc into chain spaces made on previous rounds. These groups of 3dc are often called 3dc-clusters or 3dc-groups. They are often separated by working 1 chain between the 3dc-groups, and they create the classic granny stitch.
- A square is created by working more stitches into the corners. In a classic granny square, this is two 3dc-groups into the corner, separated by 2 chains. These 2 chains form the corner space.
- To begin your square, you will chain 5 and slip stitch into the first of these 5 chain to form a ring (see Starting with a Chain Ring). This is the easiest method for a beginner to start their first square.

Yarn

You can use any yarn thickness to create your squares (see All About Size)

Hook

Use the hook size recommended for the yarn you are using

Extras

- Removable stitch marker
- Yarn needle

Gauge/Tension

This will depend on the yarn and hook being used. To create the same sized squares each time, use the same yarn thickness and hook size throughout.

Abbreviations

See Techniques: Abbreviations.

CHART

STARTING WITH A CHAIN RING

The simplest way to start your first granny square is with a chain ring.

To make a chain ring, work a short length of chain stitches, then slip stitch into the first of these chain stitches to form a ring. Then you are ready to work your granny square into the center of this small ring.

1. Using the first color, make a slip knot on your hook **(A)**.

2. Ch5 **(B)**.

3. Insert the hook in the first of these 5 ch and make a slst to form a ring **(C)**.

4. Place a removable stitch marker into the center of the ring **(D)**, so that you know where to put your hook for Round 1.

You will work Round 1 into the center of the ring you have made. This ring is sometimes called a foundation ring. The right side of the square is facing, ready to work Round 1.

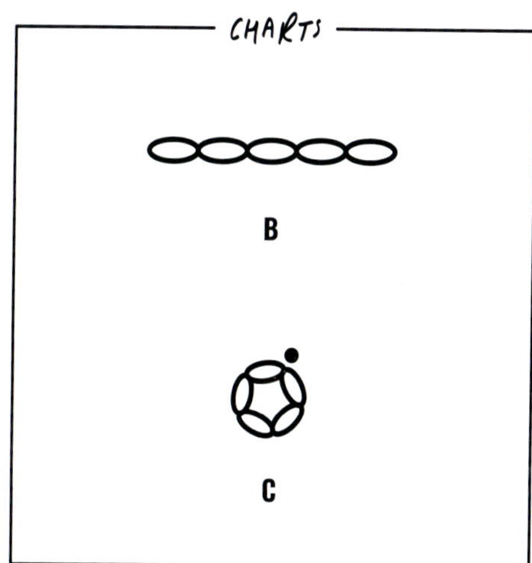

TIP FOR SUCCESS

When working your first round into the center ring, it's important to keep space for all your stitches. As you crochet, gently slide your stitches around the ring to make more room. This prevents you from accidentally crocheting over previous stitches and losing them.

WORKING ROUND 1

NOTE: *Each round will now begin with ch3. This is your beginning chain, and it consists of 3 chains, to make it the same height as a double crochet stitch. By crocheting 3 chains you will raise your hook to the correct height for working the next double crochet stitch. This beginning ch-3 always counts as your first double crochet stitch.*

Round 1 (RS): Ch3 (counts as 1dc) **(A)**, 2dc in ring **(B)**, ch2 **(C)**, [3dc in ring, ch2] 3 times **(D)**, insert hook under two loops of third ch of beginning ch-3 **(E)**, and slst to join the round **(F)**. (4 3dc-groups, 4 corner ch2-sps)

Your first round is now complete, and you have 4 groups of 3dc in your center ring, along with 4 corners that are made of ch2-sps. See the chart to identify the stitches, with the starting point of the chart shown by the ch3.

INVISIBLE FASTEN OFF

Now fasten off with an invisible fasten off as follows:

1. Remove the hook from the working loop and turn your motif over so that wrong side is facing. Insert the hook into the top of the next stitch (under both loops of stitch), to the right of the working loop **(G)**.

2. Place the working loop back on the hook **(H)**.

3. Pull the yarn tight, then pull the working loop through the top of the stitch. Cut the yarn, leaving a tail of approximately 2¾in (7cm). Yarn over hook, and pull all the way through the loop on the hook. Tighten up the knot, which will not be visible from the right side **(I)**.

4. On the wrong side, weave in your starting tail end and close up the center hole, by threading it through the base of the double crochet stitches on the wrong side **(J)**. Thread the yarn needle through the base of each stitch, then pull tight to close the hole.

5. Do the same in the opposite direction, skipping the first stitch, then inserting the yarn needle under the base of the double crochet stitches **(K)**. Pull tight and snip the yarn. Turn work to the right side.

TOP TIPS

Granny squares and motifs are a great way to use up scrap yarn. To make each motif unique, pop your yarn scraps into a bag and pull out a ball to start your motif.

1. Once you have completed the round, pop the remainder of the ball into a second bag (this ensures that you don't choose this color again for this motif).

2. Without looking into the bag, pull out another ball for the next round.

3. Once this round is complete, pop the remainder of the ball into your second bag.

Repeat Steps 2 and 3 until you reach the final round. If you choose to work the final round in the same color each time, then use this main color for the final round.

By following this method, you can make your motifs unique, and also have lots of fun with your crochet.

The right side of your work will always be facing when you start a new round. The yarn tails will help identify the wrong side of your work.

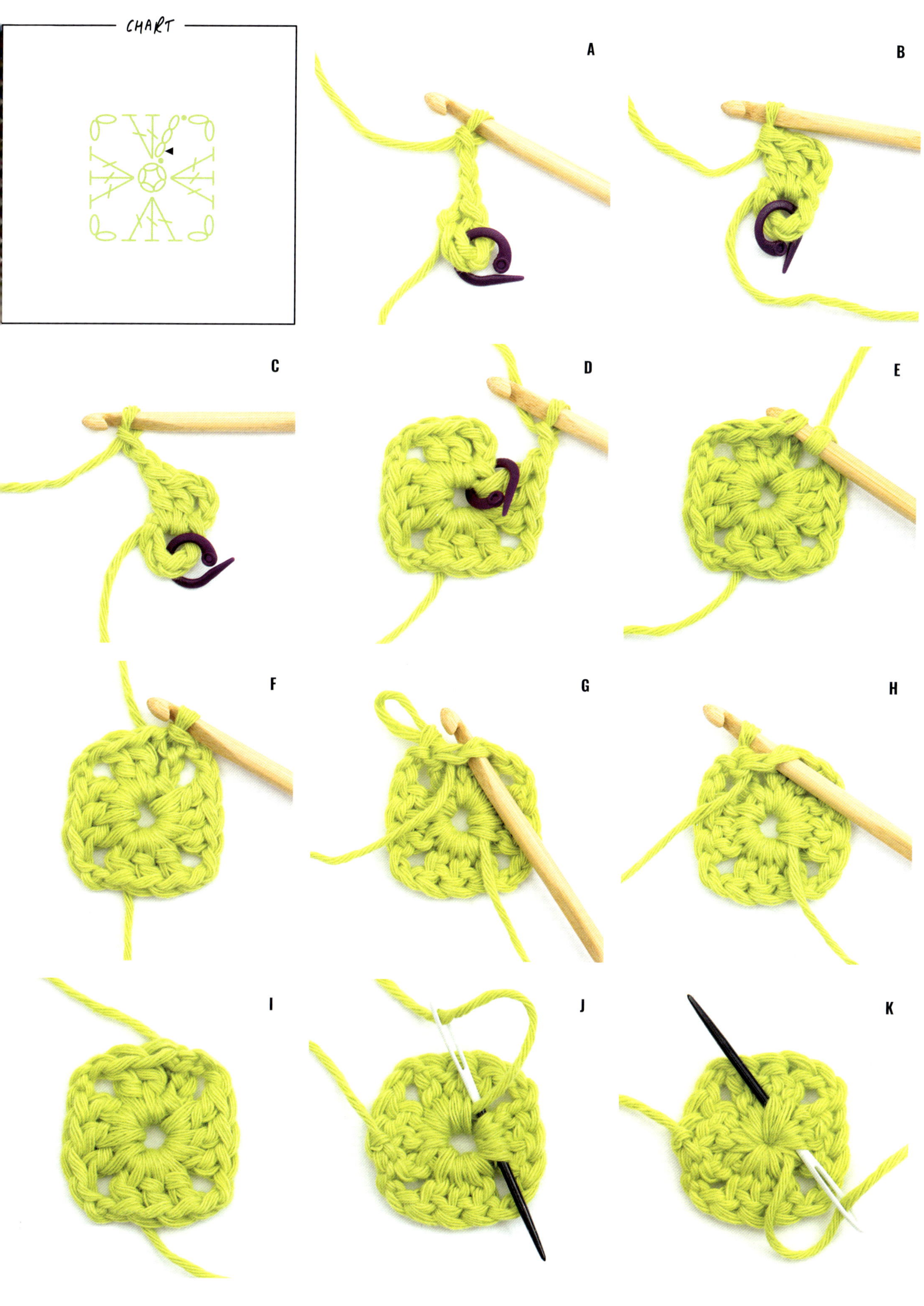
CHART
A
B
C
D
E
F
G
H
I
J
K

WORKING ROUND 2

Round 2 (RS): Join next color with slst to any corner sp, ch3 (counts as 1dc) **(L)**, [2dc, ch2, 3dc] in same corner sp, ch1 **(M)**, *[3dc, ch2, 3dc] in next corner sp, ch1; rep from * twice more **(N)**, slst in third ch of beginning ch-3 **(O)**, fasten off with invisible fasten off as before. (8 3dc-groups, 4 corner ch2-sps, 4 ch1-sps)

Your second round is now complete, and you have 4 corner groups of [3dc, ch2, 3dc], each separated along the sides by ch1-spaces.

On the wrong side, weave in your tail end of yarn from Round 1 **(P)**, and your starting tail end from Round 2 as in Steps 4 and 5 of Round 1, leaving only the fasten-off tail end from Round 2. Turn the work to the right side.

NOTE: *For ease of reading, charts often show the starting ch-3 in the same corner. To avoid all yarn ends in one spot, you can start each round in a different corner, as in all the step photos. This won't affect the final look of your square.*

L

M

N

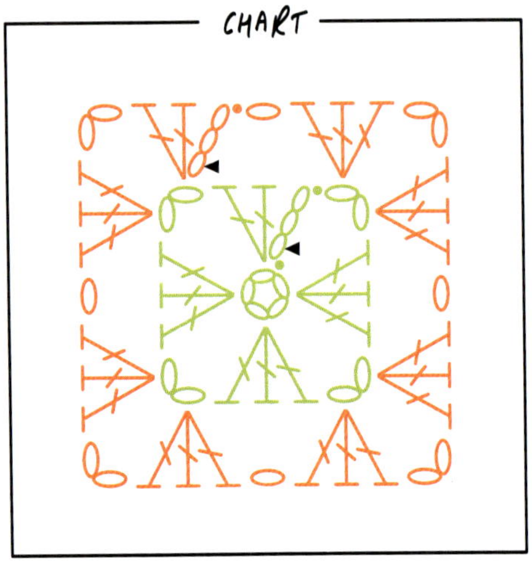

CHART

O

P

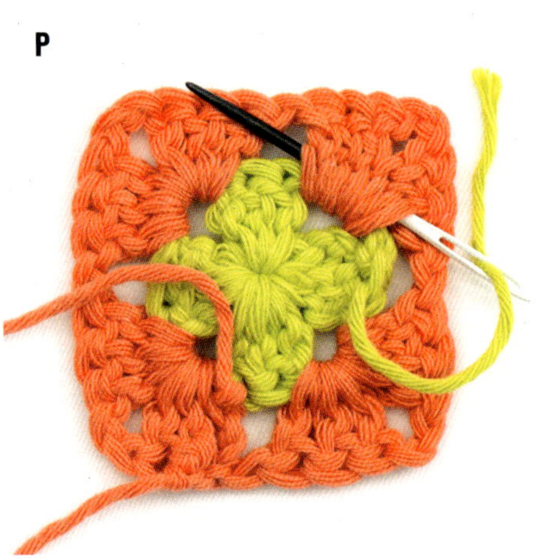

WORKING ROUND 3

Round 3 (RS): Join next color with slst to any corner sp, ch3 (counts as 1dc) **(Q)**, [2dc, ch2, 3dc] in same corner sp, ch1, 3dc in next ch1-sp, ch1 **(R)**, *[3dc, ch2, 3dc] in next corner sp, ch1, 3dc in next ch1-sp, ch1; rep from * twice more, slst in third ch of beginning ch-3 **(S)**, fasten off with invisible fasten off as before. (12 3dc-groups, 4 corner ch2-sps, 8 ch1-sps)

Your third round is now complete, and you have 4 corner groups of [3dc, ch2, 3dc], and a 3dc-group along each side, separated from the corners by ch1-sps.

On the wrong side, weave in your tail end of yarn from Round 2, and your starting tail end from Round 3, as before, leaving only the fasten-off tail end from Round 3. Turn work to the right side.

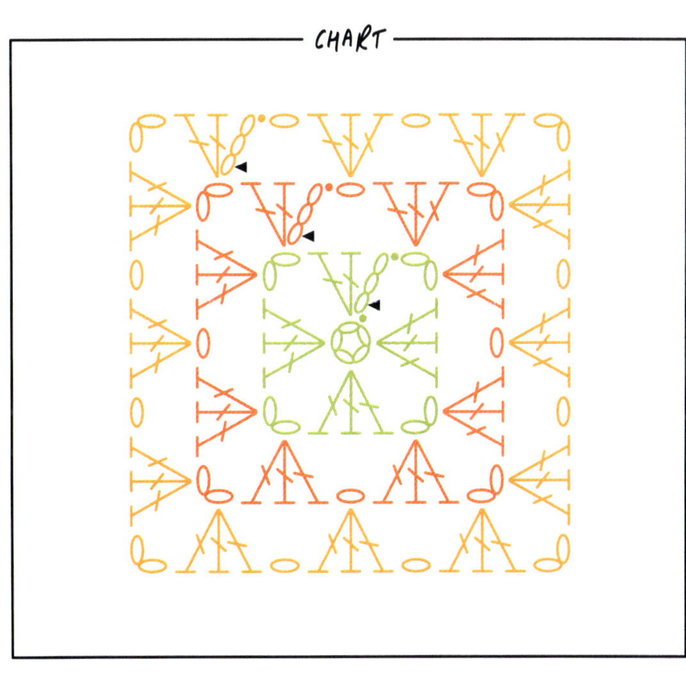

WORKING ROUND 4

Round 4 (RS): Join next color with slst to any corner sp, ch3 (counts as 1dc) **(T)**, [2dc, ch2, 3dc] in same corner sp, ch1, [3dc in next ch1-sp, ch1] to next corner **(U)**, *[3dc, ch2, 3dc] into next corner sp, ch1, [3dc in next ch1-sp, ch1] to next corner; rep from * twice more, slst in third ch of beginning ch-3 **(V)**, fasten off with invisible fasten off as before. (16 3dc-groups, 4 corner ch2-spaces, 12 ch1-spaces)

Your fourth round is now complete, and you have 4 corner groups of [3dc, ch2, 3dc], and two 3dc-groups along each side, separated by ch1-spaces.

On the wrong side, weave in your tail end of yarn from Round 3, and your starting tail end from Round 4, as before, leaving only the fasten-off tail end from Round 4. Turn work to the right side.

T

U

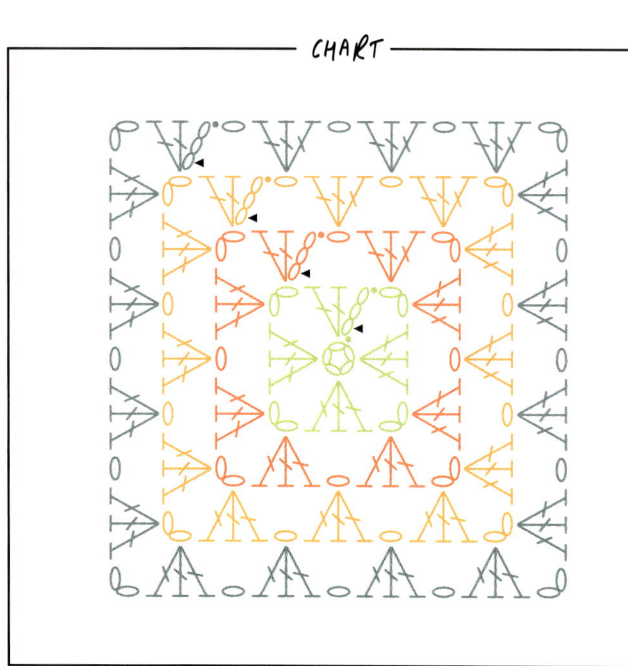

V

W

X

Y

WORKING ROUND 5

Round 5 (RS): Join next color with slst to any corner sp, ch3 (counts as 1dc) **(W)**, [2dc, ch2, 3dc] in same corner sp, ch1, [3dc in next ch1-sp, ch1] to next corner **(X)**, *[3dc, ch2, 3dc] into next corner sp, ch1, [3dc in next ch1-sp, ch1] to next corner; rep from * twice more, slst in third ch of beginning ch-3 **(Y)**, fasten off with invisible fasten off as before. (20 3dc-groups, 4 corner ch2-spaces, 16 ch1-spaces)

Your fifth round is now complete, and you have 4 corner groups of [3dc, ch2, 3dc], and three 3dc-groups along each side, separated by ch1-spaces.

On the wrong side, weave in your remaining tail ends of yarn as before, and turn the work to the right side.

The pattern of the classic granny square is now set, and you can see that there are always [3dc, ch2, 3dc] in the corners, and groups of 3dc along the sides, separated by ch1-spaces.

Continue to repeat Round 5, if desired, to add more rounds to your granny motif, and make it as big as you like.

When you have completed your square, pin it flat to block it (see Techniques: Blocking).

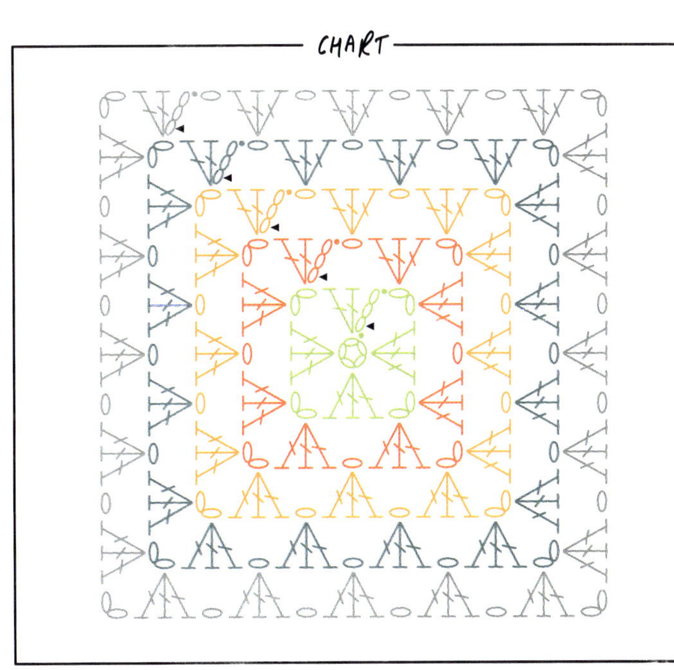

FREE SPIRIT WALL HANGINGS

This first project is really simple: fringed granny square wall hangings. They use the classic granny square, combined with a touch of rustic charm by attaching the squares to wooden sticks and adding a tassel fringe for a stylish finish. Whether you're a beginner or an experienced crocheter, this is a great project, as well as being a delightful way to bring a handmade touch to your home décor. Use your favorite colors or use colors that match your home furnishings.

YOU WILL NEED

Yarn

Scheepjes Stone Washed XL (70% cotton; 30% acrylic), worsted (aran) weight, 82yd (75m) per 1¾oz (50g) ball

Color 1: 1 ball of Beige (871 Axinite)

Color 2: 1 ball of Pale Blue (853 Amazonite)

Scheepjes River Washed XL (70% cotton; 30% acrylic), worsted (aran) weight, 82yd (75m) per 1¾oz (50g) ball

Color 3: 1 ball of Turquoise (988 Danube)

Color 4: 1 ball of Orange (982 Mississippi)

Hook

US H/8 (5mm) crochet hook

Extras

- Removable stitch marker
- Yarn needle
- Wooden dowels or sticks at least 8in (20cm) in length

Gauge/tension

Finished larger motif measures 5½ x 5½in (14 x 14cm) using US H/8 (5mm) hook and Scheepjes Stone Washed and River Washed yarns.

Finished smaller motif measures 4½ x 4½in (11.5 x 11.5cm) using US H/8 (5mm) hook and Scheepjes Stone Washed and River Washed yarns.

Finished measurements

Larger wall hanging: 5½ x 5½in (14 x 14cm) excluding fringe and hanging loop

Smaller wall hanging: 4½ x 4½in (11.5 x 11.5cm) excluding fringe and hanging loop

Abbreviations

See Techniques: Abbreviations.

PATTERN NOTES

Gauge is not critical for this project. You can use any yarn with its recommended hook size.

The square motifs are based on a classic granny square (see Multi-Color Classic Granny Square).

PATTERN BEGINS

LARGER MOTIF

Using Color 4, ch5, slst in first of these 5 ch to form a ring (see Motif 1: Starting with a Chain Ring). Alternatively, you can start with a magic ring (see Techniques).

You will now work Round 1 into the ring you have made.

Place a removable stitch marker in the center of the ring so you know where to put your hook for Round 1.

Round 1 (RS): Ch3 (counts as 1dc), 2dc in ring, ch2, [3dc in ring, ch2] 3 times, slst in third ch of beginning ch-3. (4 3dc-groups, 4 corner ch2-sps)

Fasten off with invisible fasten off.

Round 2 (RS): Join Color 2 with slst to any corner sp, ch3 (counts as 1dc), [2dc, ch2, 3dc] in same corner sp, ch1, *[3dc, ch2, 3dc] in next corner sp, ch1; rep from * twice more, slst in third ch of beginning ch-3. (8 3dc-groups, 4 corner ch2-sps, 4 ch1-sps)

Fasten off with invisible fasten off.

Round 3 (RS): Join Color 1 with slst to any corner sp, ch3 (counts as 1dc), [2dc, ch2, 3dc] in same corner sp, ch1, 3dc in next ch1-sp, ch1, *[3dc, ch2, 3dc] in next corner sp, ch1, 3dc in next ch1-sp, ch1; rep from * twice more, slst in third ch of beginning ch3. (12 3dc-groups, 4 corner ch2-sps, 8 ch1-sps)

Fasten off with invisible fasten off.

Round 4 (RS): Join Color 4 with slst to any corner sp, ch3 (counts as 1dc), [2dc, ch2, 3dc] in same corner sp, ch1, [3dc in next ch1-sp, ch1] to next corner, *[3dc, ch2, 3dc] in next corner sp, ch1, [3dc in next ch1-sp, ch1] to next corner; rep from * twice more, slst in third ch of beginning ch-3. (16 3dc-groups, 4 corner ch2-sps, 12 ch1-sps)

Fasten off with invisible fasten off.

Round 5 (RS): Using Color 3, rep Round 4. (20 3dc-groups, 4 corner ch2-sps, 16 ch1-sps)

Round 6 (edging): With RS facing, join Color 1 with slst to any corner sp, ch1 (does not count as a st), [1sc, ch2, 1sc] in same corner sp, 1sc in each st and sp to next corner, *[1sc, ch2, 1sc] in next corner sp, 1sc in each st and sp to next corner; rep from * twice more, slst in first sc. (84 sc, 4 corner ch2-sps)

Fasten off with invisible fasten off. Weave in ends on the wrong side.

Make a second Larger Motif, using Color 1 for Round 1, Round 4 and Round 6; Color 3 for Round 2; Color 4 for Round 3; Color 2 for Round 5.

SMALLER MOTIF

Work as given for Larger Motif to end of Round 4, using Color 3 for Round 1; Color 4 for Round 2; Color 2 for Round 3; Color 1 for Round 4.

Next round (edging): Using Color 4, work as given for Round 6 (edging) of Larger Motif. (68 sc, 4 corner ch2-sps)

Fasten off with invisible fasten off. Weave in ends on the wrong side.

FRINGE

For all motifs, use the same color as the edging round for the fringe (or you can use all colors to create a colorful fringe if preferred).

For the Smaller Motifs cut thirty 14¼in (36cm) lengths of yarn. Use three lengths of yarn for each fringe tassel.

For the Larger Motifs cut forty-eight 17¼in (44cm) lengths of yarn. Use four lengths of yarn for each fringe tassel.

Hold the lengths of yarn together and fold in half. With the right side of the motif facing, insert the hook from back to front in the bottom right corner stitch on the motif, place the folded yarn over the hook and pull through for approximately 1in (2.5cm) to form a loop. Thread the ends of the yarn through the loop and pull tight.

Continue to attach fringe tassels across the bottom edge of the motif, working through every alternate stitch approximately, making sure to end with a fringe in the opposite corner space. Trim the fringe to create a straight line.

ATTACH TO STICK

Using the same color as the edging round, make a slip knot on the hook. With the right side facing, join yarn with slst in the top right-hand corner space, place the wooden stick along the working edge and on top of the working yarn, take yarn over hook **(A)** and pull through.

Now work single crochet through every stitch along the top of the motif, inserting the hook in the stitch and under the wooden stick to trap it into the stitches, yarn over hook and pull loop through to front **(B)**. Lengthen the stitch to bring it in line with the top of the wooden stick, yarn over hook and pull through to complete the single crochet. End with a single crochet in the opposite corner.

Fasten off and weave in ends on the wrong side.

HANGING LOOP

Using the same color as the edging round, make a slip knot on the hook. With the right side facing, join with a slip stitch to the sixth stitch from the right-hand end of the wooden stick. Make a chain to the hanging length required then slip stitch in the sixth stitch from the left-hand end.

Working back along the chain just made, work a slip stitch in each chain to create a firm hanging loop that doesn't stretch.

Fasten off and weave in ends on the wrong side.

A

B

MOTIF 2: SINGLE-COLOR CLASSIC GRANNY SQUARE

To work your granny square motif in a single color throughout, there is no need to fasten off your yarn after every round and re-join a new color. Instead, you continue with the same yarn.

But there is one extra step required for each round, because you need to move your hook along from the join to the starting corner for the next round. This process is fully explained in the instructions. It may seem odd at first, but you'll soon get the hang of it, and it's a great way to work because the extra slip stitches help to strengthen the joining area and keep your square looking straight.

Yarn

You can use any yarn thickness to create your squares (see All About Size)

Hook

Use the hook size recommended for the yarn you are using

Extras

- Removable stitch marker
- Yarn needle

Gauge/Tension

This will depend on the yarn and hook being used. To create the same sized squares each time, use the same yarn thickness and hook size throughout.

Abbreviations

See Techniques: Abbreviations.

CHART

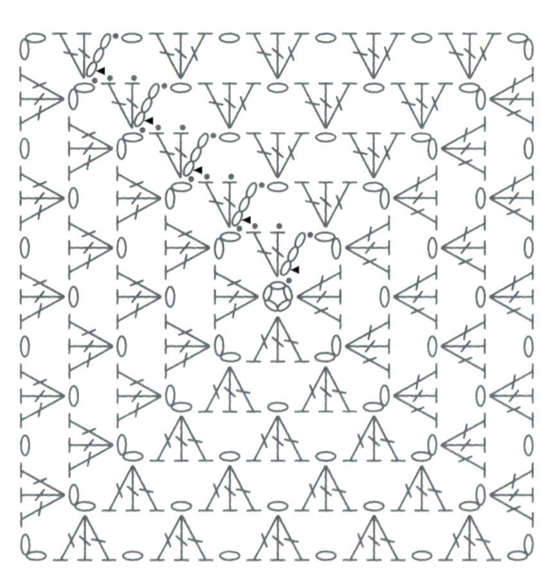

PATTERN

Ch5, slst in first of these 5 ch to form a ring (see Motif 1: Starting with a Chain Ring).

Place a removable stitch marker into the center of the ring so you know where to put your hook for Round 1.

Round 1 (RS): Ch3 (counts as 1dc), 2dc in ring, ch2, [3dc in ring, ch2] 3 times **(A)**, insert hook under two loops of the third ch of beginning ch-3 **(B)**, and slst to join round. (4 3dc-groups, 4 corner ch2-spaces)

Slst in each of next 2 dc **(C)**, to move hook along sts **(D)**. Slst in corner space, so hook is in correct place to start next round **(E)**.

Round 2 (RS): Ch3 (counts as 1dc) **(F)**, [2dc, ch2, 3dc] in same corner sp, ch1, *[3dc, ch2, 3dc] in next corner sp, ch1; rep from * twice more, slst in third ch of beginning ch-3, slst in each of next 2 dc, slst in corner ch2-sp. (8 3dc-groups, 4 corner ch2-sps, 4 ch1-sps)

Round 3 (RS): Ch3 (counts as 1dc), [2dc, ch2, 3dc] in same corner sp, ch1, 3dc in next ch1-sp, ch1, *[3dc, ch2, 3dc] in next corner sp, ch1, 3dc in next ch1-sp, ch1; rep from * twice more, slst in third ch of beginning ch-3, slst in each of next 2 dc, slst in corner ch2-sp. (12 3dc-groups, 4 corner ch2-sps, 8 ch1-sps)

Round 4 (RS): Ch3 (counts as 1dc), [2dc, ch2, 3dc] in same corner sp, ch1, [3dc in next ch1-sp, ch1] to next corner, *[3dc, ch2, 3dc] in next corner sp, ch1, [3dc in next ch1-sp, ch1] to next corner sp; rep from * twice more, slst in third ch of beginning ch-3, slst in each of next 2 dc, slst in corner ch2-sp. (16 3dc-groups, 4 corner ch2-sps, 12 ch1-sps)

Round 5 (RS): As Round 4 but fasten off with invisible fasten off after joining the round. (20 3dc-groups, 4 corner ch2-sps, 16 ch1-sps)

Weave in ends on wrong side.

The pattern of the single-color classic granny square is now set, and you can see that there are always [3dc, ch2, 3dc] in the corners, and groups of 3dc along the sides, separated by ch1-sps.

To make your square larger, do not fasten off after Round 5—instead slst in the next 2 dc and in the corner ch2-sp, then continue to repeat Round 4 to add more rounds.

To finish, pin your square flat to block it (see Techniques: Blocking).

NOTE: *With these two basic granny squares (multi-color and single color) you can make endless combinations of squares. Whip stitch the squares to join, or use a slip stitch seam on the wrong side (see Joining Techniques).*

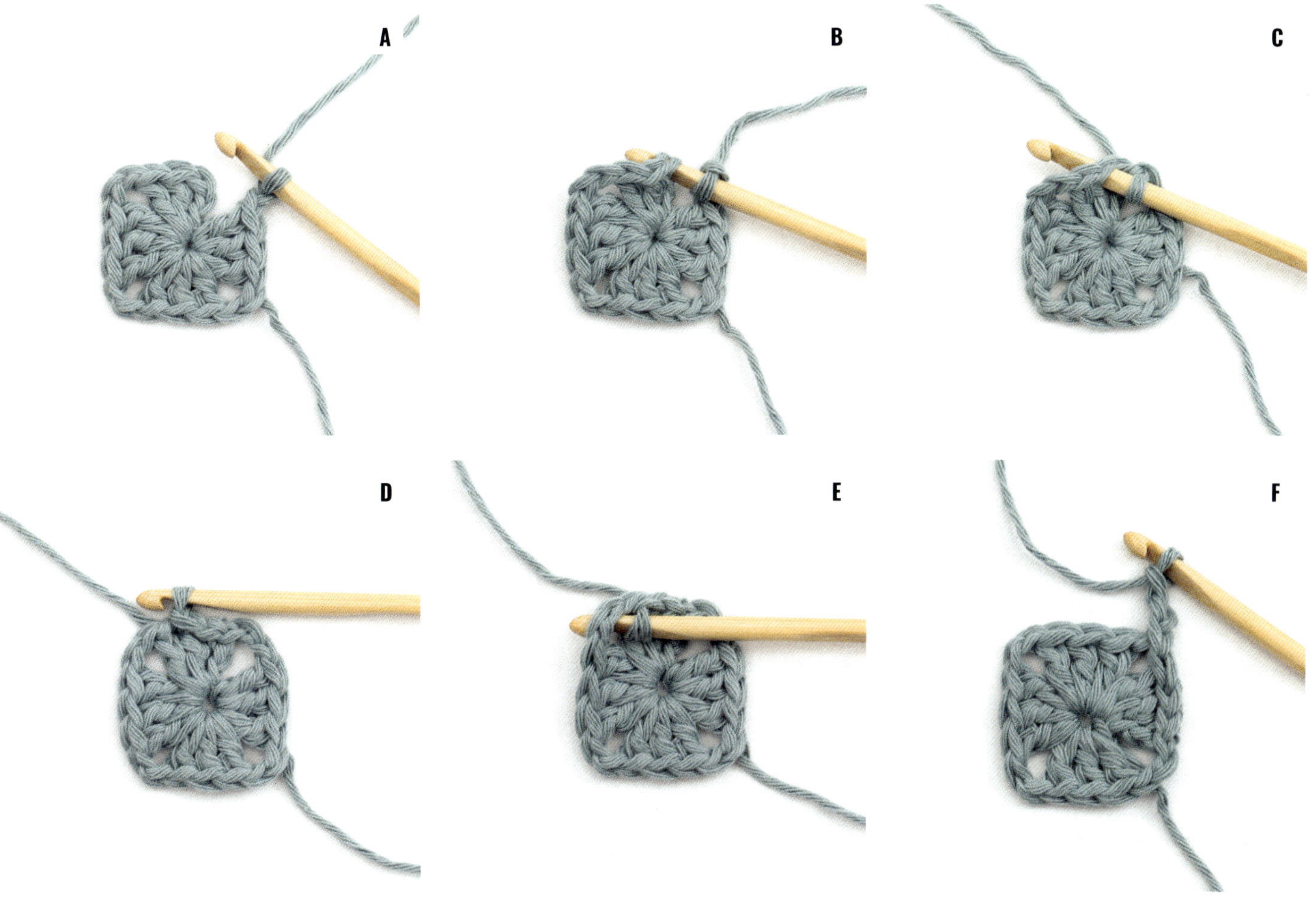

SWEET AND SIMPLE LAP BLANKET

This large, colorful granny square is an ideal pattern for beginners, and the multi-colored yarn means there's no need for color changes. It's the perfect project for practicing granny square crochet, and you'll finish with a beautiful blanket that would make a great gift for a newborn. The process of creating can be thoroughly enjoyed, as you find your flow in the relaxing and calming rhythm of the granny stitch.

YOU WILL NEED

Yarn

Scheepjes Stone Washed Minerals (78% cotton; 22% acrylic), sport weight (5ply), 142yd (130m) per 1¾oz (50g) ball

Color 1: 6 balls of Opal Ocean (906)

Scheepjes Stone Washed (70% cotton; 30% acrylic), sport weight (5ply), 142yd (130m) per 1¾oz (50g) ball

Color 2: 1 ball of Deep Amethyst (811)

Hook

US G/6 (4mm) crochet hook

Extras

- Removable stitch marker
- Yarn needle

Gauge/tension

8.5 rounds and 5 pattern repeats of [3dc, ch1] measure 4 x 4in (10 x 10cm) using US G/6 (4mm) hook and Scheepjes Stone Washed Minerals.

Finished measurements

Approximately 32 x 32in (81.5 x 81.5cm)

Abbreviations

See Techniques: Abbreviations.

PATTERN NOTES

Gauge is not critical for this project.

The square motif is based on a classic granny square (see Single-color Classic Granny Square).

PATTERN BEGINS

BLANKET

Using Color 1, ch5, slst in first of these 5 ch to form a ring (see Motif 1: Starting with a Chain Ring). Alternatively, you can start with a magic ring (see Techniques).

You will now work Round 1 into the ring you have made.

Place a removable stitch marker into the center of the ring so you know where to put your hook for Round 1.

Round 1 (RS): Ch3 (counts as 1dc here and throughout), 2dc in ring, ch2, [3dc in ring, ch2] 3 times, slst in third ch of beginning ch-3, slst in each of next 2 dc, slst in corner ch2-sp. (4 3dc-groups, 4 corner ch2-sps)

Round 2 (RS): Ch3, [2dc, ch2, 3dc] in same corner sp, ch1, *[3dc, ch2, 3dc] in next corner sp, ch1; rep from * twice more, slst in third ch of beginning ch-3, slst in each of next 2 dc, slst in corner ch2-sp. (8 3dc-groups, 4 corner ch2-sps, 4 ch1-sps)

Round 3 (RS): Ch3, [2dc, ch2, 3dc] in same corner sp, ch1, 3dc in next ch1-sp, ch1, *[3dc, ch2, 3dc] in next corner sp, ch1, 3dc in next ch1-sp, ch1; rep from * twice more, slst in third ch of beginning ch-3, slst in each of next 2 dc, slst in corner ch2-sp. (12 3dc-groups, 4 corner ch2-sps, 8 ch1-sps)

Round 4 (RS): Ch3 (counts as 1dc), [2dc, ch2, 3dc] in same corner sp, ch1, [3dc in next ch1-sp, ch1] to next corner, *[3dc, ch2, 3dc] in next corner sp, ch1, [3dc in next ch1-sp, ch1] to next corner; rep from * twice more, slst in third ch of beginning ch-3, slst in each of next 2 dc, slst in corner ch2-sp. (16 3dc-groups, 4 corner ch2-sps, 12 ch1-sps)

Rounds 5–34: Rep Round 4.

Fasten off at the end of Round 34, and weave in ends on the wrong side. You will have 34 3dc-groups along each side separated by ch1-sps, and 4 corner ch2-sps.

BORDER

See Borders: Shell Stitch Border for a chart of this border.

Round 1 (RS): Join Color 2 with slst in any corner sp, ch3 (counts as first dc), 4dc in same corner sp, work 1dc in every st and ch1-sp to next corner, *5dc in corner, work 1dc in every st and ch1-sp to next corner; rep from * twice more, slst in third ch of beginning ch-3 to join. (135 dc along each side, 5 dc in each corner; 560 dc in total)

Fasten off Color 1 with invisible fasten off.

Round 2 (RS): Join Color 1 with slst in first dc of any corner, *ch5, skip next 3 dc, slst in next dc; rep from * to last 3 dc, 5ch, skip next 3 dc, slst in base of beginning ch-5. (140 ch5-loops)

Fasten off Color 2.

Round 3 (RS): Join Color 2 with slst to any ch5-sp, ch1 (does not count as a st) *[1sc, 1hdc, 1dc, ch2, 1dc, 1hdc, 1sc] all in ch5-sp (working over the ch5-loop and not into any individual sts); rep from * in every ch5-sp to end, slst in first sc. (140 shells)

Fasten off, weave in ends on wrong side.

FINISHING

Pin flat, spray block and leave to dry completely.

MOTIF 3: GRANNY TRIANGLE

Triangle granny motifs offer a fresh twist on the classic square, adding interest to your crochet projects. With their three sides, triangular motifs can be used to create distinctive patterns, fill gaps in larger projects, or add decorative elements to your designs. Whether you're making a shawl, a scarf, or an intricate blanket, granny triangles provide endless possibilities to create unique projects.

GRANNY TRIANGLE FACTS

- To begin your triangle, you will chain 5 and slip stitch into the first of these 5 chain to form a ring (see Motif 1: Starting with a Chain Ring). This is the easiest method for a beginner to start their first triangle. Alternatively, you can start with a magic ring (see Techniques).
- The first round is formed with a center of three 3dc-groups, separated by chain spaces.
- The chain spaces in a triangle motif have an additional chain, to help keep the motif flat. Each corner has a ch3-sp, with ch2-sps along the sides between the dc groups.

Yarn

You can use any yarn thickness to create your squares (see All About Size)

Hook

Use the hook size recommended for the yarn you are using

Extras

- Removable stitch marker
- Yarn needle

Gauge/Tension

This will depend on the yarn and hook being used. To create the same sized squares each time, use the same yarn thickness and hook size throughout.

Abbreviations

See Techniques: Abbreviations.

CHART

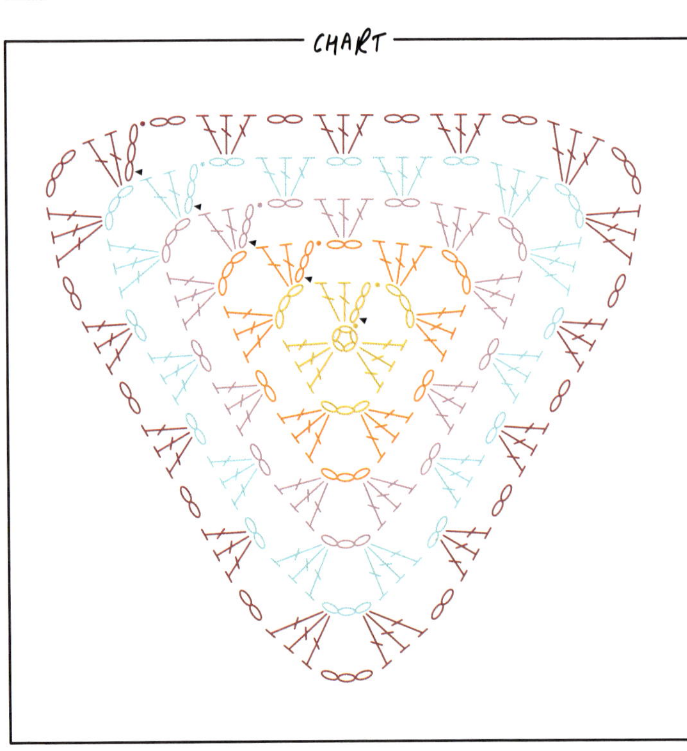

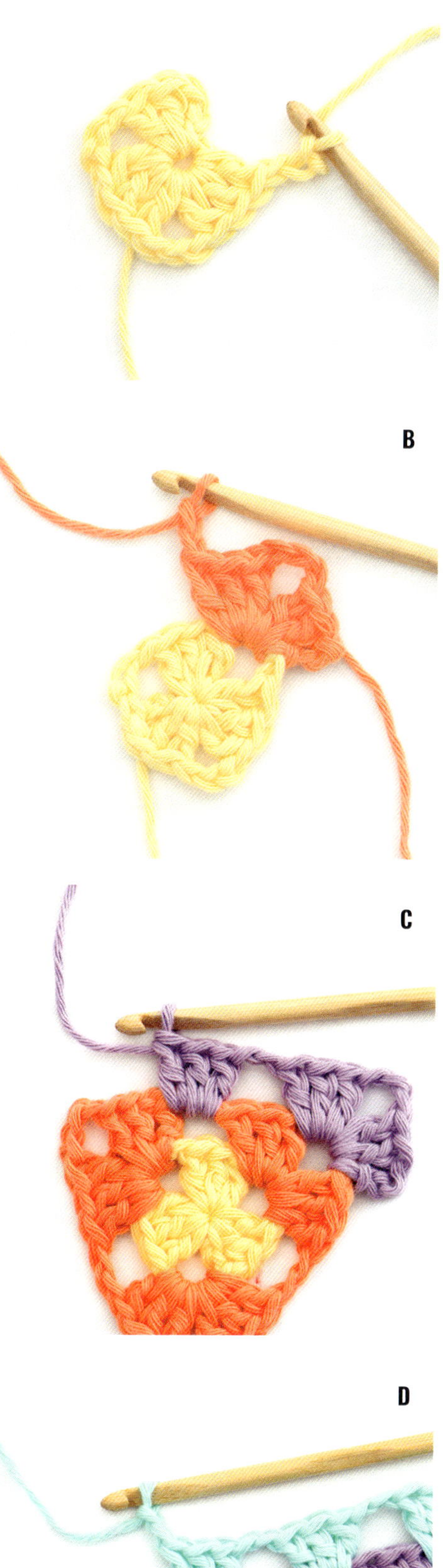

PATTERN

Using first color, ch5, slst in first of these 5 ch to form a ring (see Motif 1: Starting with a Chain Ring).

Place a removable stitch marker into the center of the ring so you know where to put your hook for Round 1.

Round 1 (RS): Ch3 (counts as 1dc), 2dc in ring, ch3, [3dc in ring, ch3] twice **(A)**, slst in third ch of beginning ch-3. (3 3dc-groups, 3 ch3-sps)

Fasten off with invisible fasten off.

You can join the yarn to any corner to start each round.

Round 2 (RS): Join next color with slst to any ch3-sp, ch3 (counts as 1dc), [2dc, ch3, 3dc] in same ch3-sp, ch2 **(B)**, *[3dc, ch3, 3dc] in next ch3-sp, ch2; rep from * once more, slst in third ch of beginning ch-3. (6 3dc-groups, 3 ch3-sps, 3 ch2-sps)

Fasten off with invisible fasten off.

Round 3 (RS): Join next color with slst to any ch3-sp, ch3 (counts as 1dc), [2dc, ch3, 3dc] in same ch3-sp, ch2, 3dc in next ch2-sp **(C)**, ch2, *[3dc, ch3, 3dc] in next ch3-sp, ch2, 3dc in next ch2-sp, ch2; rep from * once more, slst in third ch of beginning ch-3. (9 3dc-groups, 3 ch3-sps, 6 ch2-sps)

Fasten off with invisible fasten off.

Round 4 (RS): Join next color with slst to any ch3-sp, ch3 (counts as 1dc), [2dc, ch3, 3dc] in same ch3-sp, ch2, [3dc in next ch2-sp, ch2] to next corner ch3-sp, *[3dc, ch3, 3dc] in next ch3-sp, ch2, [3dc in next ch2-sp, ch2] to next corner ch3-sp; rep from * once more **(D)**, slst in third ch of beginning ch-3. (12 3dc-groups, 3 ch3-sps, 9 ch2-sps)

Fasten off with invisible fasten off.

Round 5 (RS): Using next color, work as Round 4. (15 3dc-groups, 3 ch3-sps, 12 ch2-sps)

Continue to rep Round 4, if desired, to add more rounds to your triangle motif.

Fasten off with invisible fasten off, weave in ends on wrong side.

SINGLE-COLOR GRANNY TRIANGLE

To work your triangle motif in a single color throughout, there is no need to fasten off your yarn after every round and re-join a new color. Instead, continue with the same yarn throughout as follows:

As with the classic granny square, after joining each round, slst into each of the next 2 dc and slst into the corner ch-sp, ready to start the next round.

VIVID RAINBOW TRIANGLE BUNTING

This striking design is based on the triangle motif, with two additional rounds of edging. You can use vivid colors and make a bright decoration to brighten up your favorite room or your outdoor space, or you could choose neutral or pastel shades for a calming feel. As with most granny square projects, this is the perfect project for using up stash yarn, as only small amounts are needed for each round.

YOU WILL NEED

Yarn

Scheepjes Softfun (60% cotton; 40% acrylic), light worsted (DK) weight, 153yd (140m) per 1¾oz (50g) ball

Color 1: 1 ball of Candy Apple (2410)

Color 2: l ball of Pumpkin (2651)

Color 3: 1 ball of Bumblebee (2634)

Color 4: 1 ball of Emerald (2605)

Color 5: 1 ball of Cool Blue (2603)

Color 6: 1 ball of Deep Violet (2515)

Color 7: 1 ball of Pink (2480)

Hook

US E/4 (3.5mm) crochet hook

Extras

- Removable stitch marker
- Yarn needle

Gauge/tension

Each motif measures 6¼ x 6¼in (16 x 16cm) using US E/4 (3.5mm) hook and Scheepjes Softfun.

Finished measurements

With ten motifs, finished strip of bunting is approximately 84in (2.15m) long, but can be made to desired length

Abbreviations

See Techniques: Abbreviations.

PATTERN NOTES

This bunting is made up of individual triangle motifs crocheted together to form a long length of bunting.

Note that only small amounts of each color are used, approximately ¾oz (20g) of each to make ten motifs with tassels. If preferred, you could use Scheepjes Softfun color pack in Rainbow, which has twelve ¾oz (20g) balls.

You can use oddments of light worsted (DK) yarn, or use the yarn specified.

Gauge is not critical for this project.

PATTERN BEGINS

TRIANGLE MOTIF

(make 10, with colors in order of Red, Orange, Yellow, Green Blue, Purple, Pink)

Start each motif with a different color for Round 1, then continue in the color sequence. For example a motif with Purple as Round 1 will have a color sequence of Purple, Pink, Red, Orange, Yellow, Green, Blue.

Using chosen color for first round, ch5, slst in first of these 5 ch to form a ring (see Motif 1: Starting with a Chain Ring). Alternatively, you can start with a magic ring (see Techniques).

You will now work Round 1 into the ring you have made.

Place a removable stitch marker into the center of the ring so you know where to put your hook for Round 1.

Round 1 (RS): Ch3 (counts as 1dc), 2dc into ring, ch3, [3dc into ring, ch3] twice, slst in third ch of beginning ch-3. (3 3dc-groups, 3 ch3-sps)

Fasten off with invisible fasten off.

Round 2 (RS): Join next color with slst to any corner ch3-sp, ch3 (counts as 1dc), [2dc, ch3, 3dc] into same ch3-sp, ch2, *[3dc, ch3, 3dc] into next ch3-sp, ch2; rep from * once more, slst in third ch of beginning ch-3. (6 3dc-groups, 3 ch3-sps, 3 ch2-sps)

Fasten off with invisible fasten off.

Round 3 (RS): Join next color with slst to any corner ch3-sp, ch3 (counts as 1dc), [2dc, ch3, 3dc] into same ch3-sp, ch2, [3dc in next ch2-sp, ch2] twice, *[3dc, ch3, 3dc] into next ch3-sp, ch2, [3dc in next ch2-sp, ch2] twice; rep from * once more, slst in third ch of beginning ch-3. (9 3dc-groups, 3 ch3-sps, 6 ch2-sps)

Fasten off with invisible fasten off.

Round 4 (RS): Join next color with slst to any corner ch3-sp, ch3 (counts as 1dc), [2dc, ch3, 3dc] into same ch3-sp, ch2, [3dc in next ch2-sp, ch2] to next corner ch3-sp, *[3dc, ch3, 3dc] into corner ch3-sp, ch2, [3tr in next ch2-sp, ch2] to next corner ch3-sp; rep from * once more, slst in third ch of beginning ch-3. (12 3dc-groups, 3 ch3-sps, 9 ch2-sps)

Fasten off with invisible fasten off.

Round 5 (RS): With next color, work as Round 4. (15 3dc-groups, 3 ch3-sps, 12 ch2-sps)

Fasten off with invisible fasten off.

Round 6 (RS): Join next color with slst to any corner ch3-sp, ch1 (does not count as a st), *[2hdc, ch3, 2hdc] in corner ch3-sp, 1hdc in next 3 dc, [2hdc in next ch2-sp, 1hdc in next 3 dc] to next corner ch3-sp; rep from * to end, slst in first hdc. (81 hdc, 3 ch3-sps)

Fasten off with invisible fasten off.

Round 7 (RS): Join next color with slst to any corner ch3-sp, ch1 (does not count as a st), *[2sc, ch2, 2sc] in corner ch3-sp, 1sc in each st to next corner ch3-sp; rep from * to end, slst in first sc. (93 sc, 3 ch2-sps)

Fasten off with invisible fasten off, weave in ends on wrong side.

TASSELS

For each motif, make a tassel (see Techniques: Making a Tassel) using the same color of yarn as for the outside edge.

Sew the tassel to the bunting flag at the bottom tip, using the yarn ends from the top of the tassel.

Pin each motif flat and spray with cold water, including tassel. Leave to dry completely.

JOINING

The bunting flags are joined with rows of slip stitch, which creates a great cord effect. Lay out the motifs in a row, in a pleasing order.

Row 1 (RS): Using any color of your choice, make 40ch, then join first triangle as follows: *1hdc in right-hand top corner of triangle motif, 1hdc in next st, make 15ch, skip 14 sts, 1hdc in center st **(A)**, make 15ch, skip 14 sts, 1hdc in last st along the top edge of same triangle, 1hdc in corner sp, make 4ch **(B)**; rep from * until all bunting flags are joined, then work a further 36ch (to complete final 40ch).

Fasten off. Do not turn work.

Row 2 (RS): Join any color of your choice to first st of Row 1, work 1slst in each st to end.

NOTE: *Make sure when you work into each of the chain stitches from Row 1 that you keep the smooth (flat) side of the chain facing you, and that you work into the top loop of the chain stitches only. When you reach the hdc stitches, work into the back loop of these stitches only.*

Fasten off. Do not turn work.

Row 3 (RS): Join any color of your choice, work as given for Row 2, but work each slst in the Row 1 loops that are sitting behind Row 2 sts.

Fasten off.

FINISHING

Weave remaining ends into wrong side and trim.

Block bunting again if desired.

A

B

MOTIF 4: GRANNY HEXAGON

The hexagon motif offers a modern shape that can be used to create stunning geometric patterns. With its six sides, the hexagon opens up a world of possibilities for unique designs, whether you're crafting a colorful blanket, a stylish bag, or an eye-catching garment. Its adaptable nature allows for endless creativity in color combinations and stitch variations, making the hexagon motif a firm favorite for both beginners and experienced crocheters alike.

GRANNY HEXAGON FACTS

- To begin your hexagon, chain 5 and slip stitch into the first of these 5 ch to form a ring (see Motif 1: Starting with a Chain Ring). This is the easiest method for a beginner to start their first hexagon. Alternatively, you can start with a magic ring (see Techniques).
- The first round is formed with a center of 6 dc-groups, separated by chain spaces.
- These dc-groups are made of 2 dc (and not 3 dc as in a classic granny square). Because there are more sides and therefore more stitches along each edge, only 2 dc are needed in each group throughout the motif, to help keep it flat.

Yarn

You can use any yarn thickness to create your squares (see All About Size)

Hook

Use the hook size recommended for the yarn you are using

Extras

- Removable stitch marker
- Yarn needle

Gauge/Tension

This will depend on the yarn and hook being used. To create the same sized squares each time, use the same yarn thickness and hook size throughout.

Abbreviations

See Techniques: Abbreviations.

CHART

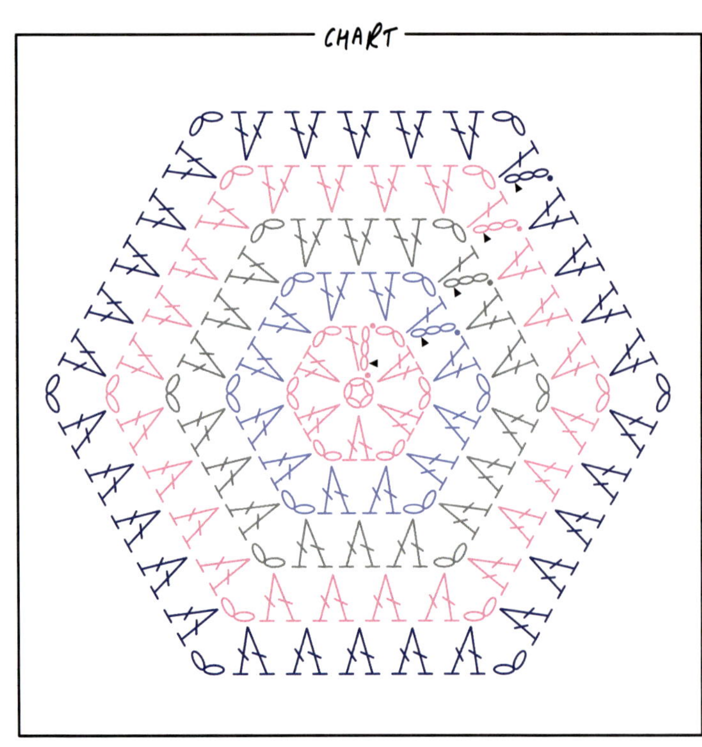

A

B

C

D

PATTERN

Using first color, ch5, slst in first of these 5 ch to form a ring (see Motif 1: Starting with a Chain Ring).

Place a removable stitch marker into the center of the ring so you know where to put your hook for Round 1.

Round 1 (RS): Ch3 (counts as 1dc), 1dc in ring, ch2, [2dc in ring, ch2] 5 times **(A)**, slst in third ch of beginning ch-3. (6 2dc-groups, 6 ch2-sps)

Fasten off with invisible fasten off.

You can join the yarn to any corner to start each round.

Round 2 (RS): Join next color with slst to any ch2-sp, ch3 (counts as 1dc), [1dc, ch2, 2dc] in same ch2-sp **(B)**, *[2dc, ch2, 2dc] in next ch2-sp; rep from * 4 times more, slst in third ch of beginning ch-3. (12 2dc-groups, 6 ch2-sps)

Fasten off with invisible fasten off.

Round 3 (RS): Join next color with slst to any ch2-sp, ch3 (counts as 1dc), [1dc, ch2, 2dc] in same ch2-sp, 2dc in next sp between 2dc-groups **(C)**, *[2dc, ch2, 2dc] in next ch2-sp, 2dc in next sp between 2dc-groups; rep from * 4 times more, slst in third ch of beginning ch-3. (18 2dc-groups, 6 ch2-sps)

Fasten off with invisible fasten off.

Round 4 (RS): Join next color with slst to any ch2-sp, ch3 (counts as 1dc), [1dc, ch2, 2dc] in same ch2-sp, [2dc in next sp between 2dc-groups] to next ch2-sp, *[2dc, ch2, 2dc] in next ch2-sp, [2dc in next sp between 2dc-groups] to next ch2-sp; rep from * 4 times more **(D)**, slst in third ch of beginning ch-3. (24 2dc-groups, 6 ch2-sps)

Fasten off with invisible fasten off.

Round 5 (RS): As Round 4. (30 2dc-groups, 6 ch2-sps)

Continue to rep Round 4, if desired, to add more rounds to your hexagon motif.

Fasten off with invisible fasten off, weave in ends on wrong side.

SINGLE-COLOR GRANNY HEXAGON

To work your hexagon motif in a single color throughout, there is no need to fasten off your yarn after every round and re-join a new color. Instead, continue with the same yarn throughout as follows:

As with the classic granny square, join each round with slst in third ch of beginning ch3, slst into next dc and slst into corner ch-sp, ready to start the next round.

BLUE SKIES HEXIE CARDIGAN

Start your handmade wardrobe with this stylish cardigan. You can use the colors listed or choose your favorite colors to create your own unique version. It's much easier to make than it looks, as it's based on two hexagon motifs. It's a slouchy style and very comfy to wear, and when people ask you where you got it from, you can proudly say that you made it yourself.

YOU WILL NEED

Yarn

Scheepjes Scrumptious (50% polyester; 50% acrylic), light worsted (DK) weight, 328yd (300m) per 3½oz (100g) ball

Color 1: 1 ball of Buttercream Icing (302)

Color 2: 1 ball of French Blue Macaron (343)

Color 3: 1 ball of Raspberry Rock Candy (335)

Color 4: 1 ball of Raspberry Mousse (307)

Color 5: 1 ball of Coconut Spirulina Cheesecake (342)

Color 6: 1 ball of Butterfly Pea Flower Mousse (352)

Color 7: 1 ball of Cotton Candy Meringue (330)

Color 8: 1 ball of Concord Grape Pie (356)

Color 9: 1 ball of Coconut Blueberry Muffins (378)

Color 10: 1 ball of Turkish Delight (331)

Hook

US G/6 (4mm) crochet hook

Extras

- Removable stitch marker
- Yarn needle

Gauge/tension

10.5 rounds and 5 pattern repeats of [3dc, ch1] measure 4 x 4in (10 x 10cm) using US G/6 (4mm) hook and Scheepjes Scrumptious.

Finished measurements

TO FIT CHEST:

32–34 (36–38) (40–42) (44–46) (48–50) (52–54)in

81–87 (91–97) (102–107) (112–117) (122–127) (132–137)cm

APPROX CHEST MEASUREMENTS:

43 (47) (50) (53) (56) (61)in

111 (119) (127) (135) (142) (155)cm

APPROX UPPER ARM DEPTH:

7 (7) (8) (8) (8½) (8½)in

18 (18) (19.5) (19.5) (21) (21)cm

SIDE SEAM:

10 (10½) (11) (12) (12½) (13½)in

24.5 (26.5) (28) (30) (32) (34.5)cm

Abbreviations

See Techniques: Abbreviations.

PATTERN NOTES

A variation on the granny hexagon is used, working 3dc-groups with ch1-sps throughout, instead of 2dc-groups. This creates a hexagon that doesn't sit flat. This is required in order to achieve an L-shaped piece for each half.

PATTERN BEGINS

BODY SECTION

(make 2)

Using Color 1, ch5, slst in first of these 5 ch to form a ring (see Motif 1: Starting with a Chain Ring). Alternatively, you can start with a magic ring (see Techniques).

You will now work Round 1 into the ring you have made.

Place a removable stitch marker into the center of the ring so you know where to put your hook for Round 1.

Round 1 (RS): Ch3 (counts as 1dc throughout) 2dc in ring, ch2, [3dc in ring, ch2] 5 times, slst in third ch of beginning ch-3. (6 3dc-groups, 6 ch2-sps)

Fasten off with invisible fasten off.

Round 2 (RS): Join Join Color 2 with slst in any ch2-sp, ch3, [2dc, ch2, 3dc] in same ch2-sp, ch1, [3dc, ch2, 3dc, ch1] in each ch2-sp to end, slst in third ch of beginning ch-3. (12 3dc-groups, 6 ch2-sps, 6ch1-sps)

Fasten off with invisible fasten off.

Round 3 (RS): Join Color 3 with slst in any ch2-sp, ch3, [2dc, ch2, 3dc] in same ch2-sp, ch1, [3dc, ch1] in each ch1-sp to next corner ch-sp, *[3dc, ch2, 3dc] in next corner ch-sp, ch1, [3dc, ch1] in each ch1-sp to next corner ch-sp, slst in third ch of beginning ch-3. (18 3dc- groups, 6 ch2-sps, 12 ch1-sps)

Fasten off with invisible fasten off.

A

B

FOLDING

Number each corner of your hexagon in order, from 1 to 6 around in a clockwise direction. Fold corner 1 to meet corner 2, fold corner 4 to meet corner 5, and fold corner 3 to meet corner 6. This will create an L-shaped piece for each half of the body.

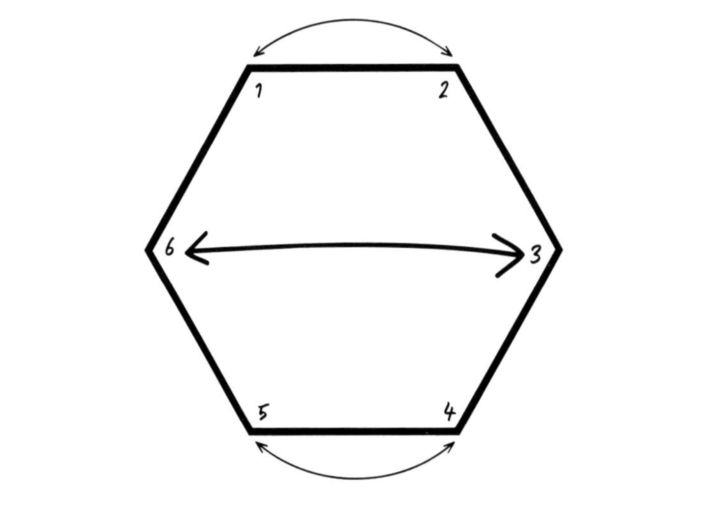

Rounds 4–21 (21, 23, 23, 25, 25): Rep Round 3, in following color sequence:

Round 4 (RS): Color 4.

Round 5 (RS): Color 1.

Round 6 (RS): Color 5.

Round 7 (RS): Color 6.

Round 8 (RS): Color 7.

Round 9 (RS): Color 1.

Round 10 (RS): Color 8.

Round 11 (RS): Color 9.

Round 12 (RS): Color 10.

Color sequence is set by Rounds 1–12.

Rounds 13–21 (21, 23, 23, 25, 25): Rep Round 3, following color sequence as set, ending with 21 (21, 23, 23, 25, 25) 3dc-groups along each side.

Fasten off with invisible fasten off, weave in ends on wrong side.

FOLDING

Fold the hexagon as in the diagram above to make an "L" shape **(A)**.

Next, sew along one of the long edges **(B)**, to create the shoulder/sleeve seam, using whip stitch (see Joining Techniques: Whip Stitch/Oversewing). Repeat for the other piece, mirroring the seam.

If you place each piece side-by-side, you will see the arms and body taking shape.

Continue both sides alike following the instructions to lengthen and widen the body.

BODY LENGTHENING AND WIDENING

Keeping color sequence correct, and with right side facing, join next color yarn in any ch-sp in line with side seam. You will now work around only three sides of piece.

Round 1 (RS): Ch3, 2dc in same ch-sp, 3dc in each ch-sp around, slst in third ch of beginning ch-3.

Fasten off with invisible fasten off.

Rounds 2–4 (6, 6, 8, 8, 12): Rep Round 1 a further 3 (5, 5, 7, 7, 11) times, maintaining color sequence.

You'll have 25 (27, 29, 31, 33, 37) rounds on both front and back.

CENTER BACK WIDENING

On left piece place a stitch marker in ch-sp in line with shoulder seam. Join next color to opposite end of center back seam, in opposite corner ch-sp to marker. (24 (26, 28, 30, 32, 36) ch1-sps between markers)

Row 1 (RS): Ch3, 1dc in same corner sp, ch1, [3dc, ch1] in each ch-sp to marked sp, 2dc in marked sp.

Fasten off. Do not turn work.

Row 2 (RS): Join next color to top of beginning ch-3 of previous row, ch4 (counts a 1dc, ch1), [3dc, ch1] in first ch-sp, [3dc, ch1] in each ch-sp to last 2 dc, skip 1 dc, 1dc in last dc.

Fasten off. Do not turn work.

Row 3 (RS): Join next color to third ch of beginning ch-4 of previous row. Ch3, 1dc in same st, ch1, skip first ch-sp and first 3dc-group, [3dc, ch1] in each ch-sp to last ch-sp, skip last ch-sp, 2dc in last dc.

Fasten off. Do not turn work.

Row 4 (RS): Rep Row 2.

Rep Center Back Widening on second piece then join center back seam with whip stitch (see Joining Techniques: Whip Stitch/Oversewing).

EDGING

Using next color in sequence, with right side facing, join Color 1 with slst in bottom corner st of left front.

It is not necessary to count your stitches for the edging rounds. If you place stitches as instructed, your edging will sit nice and flat.

Foundation round (RS): Ch1 (does not count as a st), [2sc, ch2, 2sc] in same st, 1sc in each dc to opposite end of hem (skipping the ch1-sps), work [2sc, ch2, 2sc] in corner ch2-sp. Now work along front edges and neck, as follows: 1sc in each dc and 1sc in each ch1-sp to row-ends of center back, work 2sc in each of the first 4 row-ends, 1sc in center back joining seam, then 2sc in each of the next 4 row-ends, then continue as before with 1sc in each dc and 1sc in each ch1-sp to end, slst in first sc to join, slst in next sc and slst in corner ch2-sp.

Next round (RS): Ch3 (counts as 1dc), 2dc in same corner sp, 1dcBLO in each st to next corner sp, 3dc in corner sp, 1dcBLO in each st to end, slst in top of beginning ch-3 to join, invisible fasten off.

Next round (RS): Join next color in sequence to BLO of center dc of corner stitches. Ch3 (counts as 1dc), 2dc in BLO of same st, 1dcBLO in each st to next corner st, 3dc BLO in corner st, 1dcBLO in each st to end, slst in top of beginning ch-3 to join, invisible fasten off.

If desired, you could create a deeper edging, by repeating the last round as many times as required.

Weave in ends on wrong side.

SLEEVES

Round 1 (RS): Join next color yarn to any ch sp, ch3 (counts as 1dc), 2dc in same ch-sp, ch1, [3dc, ch1] in each ch-sp around and in join of shoulder seam, slst in third ch of beginning ch-3. (22 (22, 24, 24, 26, 26) 3dc-groups and ch1-sps)

Fasten off with invisible fasten off.

Rounds 2–17: Maintaining color sequence, rep Round 1.

NOTE: *Sleeves can be lengthened or shortened by working more or fewer rows here.*

Weave in ends on wrong side.

SLEEVE CUFFS

Foundation round (RS): Join Color 1 to any ch-sp, ch3 (counts as 1dc), work 1sc in each dc (skipping the ch1-sps), slst in third ch of beginning ch-3. 66 (66, 72, 72, 78, 78) sts.

Next round (decrease round): Ch1 (does not count as a st), 1sc in first st, sc2tog, (1sc in next st, sc2tog) to end, slst in first sc. 44 (44, 48, 48, 52, 52) sts.

SLEEVE RIBBING

See Borders: Stretchy Ribbed Edge for a chart of this ribbing.

Row 1 (RS): Ch15, 1sc in second ch from hook, 1sc in each ch to end, slst in next st of decrease round, slst in following st of decrease round, turn. (14 sc)

Row 2 (WS): Skip last 2 slsts, 1scBLO in each st to last st, 1sc in last st, turn.

Row 3 (RS): Ch1 (does not count as a st), 1sc in first st, 1scBLO in next 13 sts, slst in next st of decrease round, slst in following st of decrease round.

Repeat Rows 2 and 3 around the sleeve edge, until all sts of decrease round are used up.

Fasten off.

FINISHING

Sew up ribbing seam on cuff then weave in ends on wrong side.

MOTIF 5: GRANNY OCTAGON

The octagon motif offers a distinctive shape that is different to the classic square. With its eight sides, the octagon motif creates a versatile, geometric form that lends itself beautifully to creating blankets with striking patterns. Smaller square motifs can fill the gaps between octagons, to create cohesive and harmonious patterns that offer endless opportunities for creativity.

GRANNY OCTAGON FACTS

- To begin your octagon, you will chain 5 and slip stitch into the first of these 5 ch to form a ring (see Motif 1: Starting with a Chain Ring). This is the easiest method for a beginner to start their first octagon. Alternatively, you can start with a magic ring (see Techniques).
- The first round is formed with a center of 8 dc-groups, separated by chain spaces.
- Similar to the granny hexagon, these groups are made of 2dc (and not 3dc as in a classic granny square). Because there are more sides and therefore more stitches along each edge, only 2dc are needed in each group throughout the motif, to help keep it nice and flat.

Yarn

You can use any yarn thickness to create your squares (see All About Size)

Hook

Use the hook size recommended for the yarn you are using

Extras

- Removable stitch marker
- Yarn needle

Gauge/Tension

This will depend on the yarn and hook being used. To create the same sized squares each time, use the same yarn thickness and hook size throughout.

Abbreviations

See Techniques: Abbreviations.

CHART

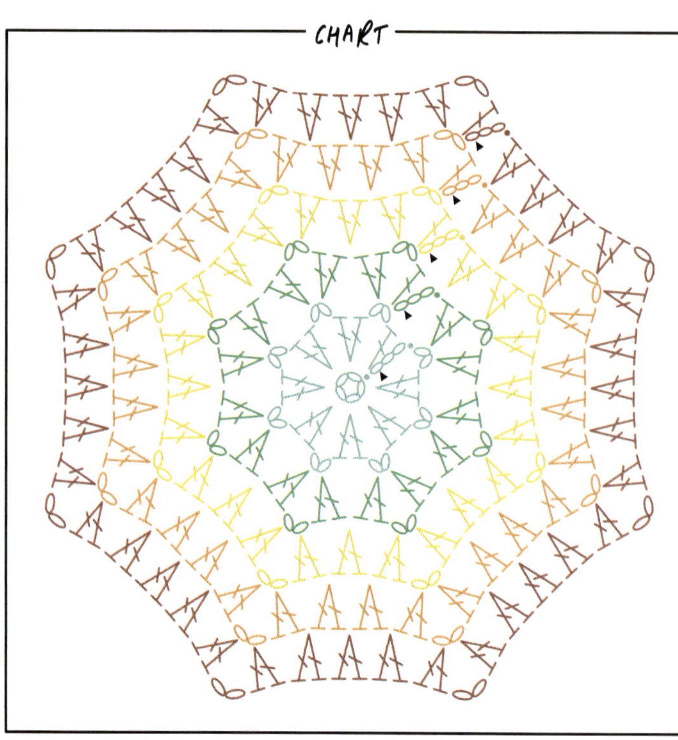

A
B

PATTERN

Using first color, ch5, slst in first of these 5 ch to form a ring (see Motif 1: Starting with a Chain Ring).

Place a removable stitch marker into the center of the ring so you know where to put your hook for Round 1.

Round 1 (RS): Ch3 (counts as 1dc), 1dc in ring, ch2, [2dc in ring, ch2] 7 times **(A)**, slst in third ch of beginning ch-3. (8 2dc-groups, 8 ch2-sps)

Fasten off with invisible fasten off.

You can join yarn to any corner to start each round.

Round 2 (RS): Join next color with slst to any ch2-sp, ch3 (counts as 1dc), [1dc, ch2, 2dc] in same ch2-sp **(B)**, *[2dc, ch2, 2dc] in next ch2-sp; rep from * 6 times more, slst in third ch of beginning ch-3. (16 2dc-groups, 8 ch2-sps)

Fasten off with invisible fasten off.

Round 3 (RS): Join next color with slst to any ch2-sp, ch3 (counts as 1dc), [1dc, ch2, 2dc] in same ch2-sp, 2dc in next sp between 2dc-groups **(C)**, *[2dc, ch2, 2dc] in next ch2-sp, 2dc in next sp between 2dc-groups; rep from * 6 times more, slst in third ch of beginning ch-3. (24 2dc-groups, 8 ch2-sps)

Fasten off with invisible fasten off.

Round 4 (RS): Join next color with slst to any ch2-sp, ch3 (counts as 1dc), [1dc, ch2, 2dc] in same ch2-sp, [2dc in next sp between 2dc-groups] to next ch2-sp, *[2dc, ch2, 2dc] in next ch2-sp, [2dc in next sp between 2dc-groups] to next ch2-sp; rep from * 6 times more **(D)**, slst in third ch of beginning ch-3. (32 2dc-groups, 8 ch2-sps)

Fasten off with invisible fasten off.

Round 5 (RS): As Round 4. (40 2dc-groups, 8 ch2-sps)

Continue to rep Round 4, if desired, to add more rounds to your octagon motif.

Fasten off with invisible fasten off, weave in ends on wrong side.

C

SINGLE-COLOR GRANNY OCTAGON

To work your octagon motif in a single color throughout, there is no need to fasten off your yarn after every round and re-join a new color. Instead, continue with the same yarn throughout as follows:

As with the hexagon motif, join each round with slst in third ch of beginning ch3, slst into the next dc and slst into the corner ch-sp, ready to start the next round.

D

OCTAGON PIN CUSHION

Using single motifs for small projects is a great way to make last-minute gifts. This pretty pin cushion is the perfect practical gift for a crafty friend, or can be a lavender pouch instead for your yarn stash, to help keep the moths at bay. It uses the octagon motif in single colors for each side, embellished with a very simple flower and leaf combination. It's perfect for using up oddments of yarn.

YOU WILL NEED

Yarn

Scheepjes Catona (100% cotton), fingering (4ply) weight, 27yd (25m) per 3/8oz (10g) ball

Color 1: 1 ball of Silver Blue (528)

Color 2: 1 ball of Saffron (249)

Color 3: 1 ball of Petrol Blue (400)

Color 4: 1 ball of Green Yellow (245)

Hook

US C/2 (2.5mm) crochet hook

Extras

- Removable stitch marker
- Yarn needle
- Small piece of plain fabric
- Sewing needle and thread
- Small amount of toy stuffing or lavender

Gauge/tension

Each motif measures 4 1/8 x 4 1/8in (10.5 x 10.5cm) using US C/2 (2.5mm) and Scheepjes Catona.

Finished measurements

Approximately 4 1/4 x 4 1/4in (11 x 11cm)

Abbreviations

See Techniques: Abbreviations.

PATTERN NOTES

Gauge is not critical for this project. You can use any yarn with its recommended hook size.

The octagon motifs are based on the basic recipe (see Granny Octagon).

PATTERN BEGINS

OCTAGON MOTIF

(make 1 in Color 1 for front, 1 in Color 2 for back)

Using chosen color, ch5, slst in first of these 5 ch to form a ring (see Motif 1: Starting with a Chain Ring). Alternatively, you can start with a magic ring (see Techniques).

You will now work Round 1 into the ring you have made.

Place a removable stitch marker into the center of the ring so you know where to put your hook for Round 1.

Round 1 (RS): Ch3 (counts as 1dc), 1dc in ring, ch2, [2dc in ring, ch2] 7 times, slst in third ch of beginning ch-3, slst in next dc, slst in ch2-sp. (8 2dc-groups, 8 ch2-sps)

Round 2 (RS): Ch3 (counts as 1dc), [1dc, ch2, 2dc] into same ch2-sp, *[2dc, ch2, 2dc] into next ch2-sp; rep from * 6 times more, slst in third ch of beginning ch-3, slst in next dc, slst in ch2-sp. (16 2dc-groups, 8 ch2-sps)

Round 3 (RS): Ch3 (counts as 1dc), [1dc, ch2, 2dc] into same ch2-sp, 2dc in next sp between 2dc-groups, *[2dc, ch2, 2dc] into next ch2-sp, 2dc in next sp between 2dc-groups; rep from * 6 times more, slst in third ch of beginning ch-3, slst in next dc, slst in ch2-sp. (24 2dc-groups, 8 ch2-sps)

Round 4 (RS): Ch3 (counts as 1dc), [1dc, ch2, 2dc] into same ch2-sp, [2dc in next sp between 2dc-groups] to next ch2-sp, *[2dc, ch2, 2dc] into next ch2-sp, [2dc in next sp between 2dc-groups] to next ch2-sp; rep from * 6 times more, slst in third ch of beginning ch-3, slst in next dc, slst in ch2-sp. (32 2dc-groups, 8 ch2-sps)

Round 5 (RS): As Round 4. (40 2dc-groups, 8 ch2-sps)

Round 6 (RS, edging): Ch1 (does not count as a st), *2sc in corner sp, 1sc in each st to next corner; rep from * 7 times more, slst in first sc. (96 sc)

Fasten off with invisible fasten off, weave in all ends on wrong side.

FLOWER EMBELLISHMENTS

FLOWER

(make 2 in Color 2, 1 in Color 3)

Using chosen color, make a magic ring.

Round 1 (RS): Ch1 (not counted as a st), *[1sc, ch2, 2dc, ch2, 1sc] into center of ring; rep from * 4 times more, slst in first sc. (5 petals made)

Cut yarn and fasten off, weave in ends on wrong side.

Tie 5 or 6 knots into center of short length of contrast yarn and thread through center of flower. Use yarn tails to sew each flower to front piece, using photo as a guide to placement.

LEAVES

(make 3)

Using Color 4, ch7.

Row 1 (RS): 1sc in second ch from hook, 1sc in next ch, 1hdc in each of next 2 ch, 1sc in each of next 2 ch.

Cut yarn and fasten off.

Use yarn tails to sew leaves between flowers.

FABRIC POUCH

Draw around one motif onto paper and cut out the shape. Use this as a template to cut two pieces of plain fabric.

With wrong sides of fabric together, whip stitch around the edges to join the pieces. Don't worry about your stitches as nobody will see them. Before joining the final edge, fill with toy stuffing or lavender, then close final edge.

FINISHING

Place front and back crochet pieces together and with front piece facing.

Join Color 2 with a slst in any st, working through both sets of stitches throughout as follows: ch1 (does not count as a st), 1sc in each st around, to join pieces. Before you join the final two edges, slide the fabric pouch inside the crochet pouch, then continue to close the seam with sc, slst in first sc to join.

Fasten off with an invisible fasten off, weave in all ends on wrong side.

TROUBLESHOOTING

Here are a few common issues that you might encounter with your granny squares, and some solutions to explain how you can fix them.

SQUARE NOT LAYING FLAT

If your granny square is curling or ruffling, it could be due to uneven gauge (tension) or incorrect stitch counts.

Solution 1: Make sure you are not adding or missing stitches in each round, and check that your gauge is consistent. Blocking the square after finishing can also help it to lay flat.

Solution 2: Change your hook size. If your square is ruffling at the edges, go down a hook size to create smaller stitches. If your edges are too tight or pulling in, go up a hook size to help loosen your stitches.

UNEVEN EDGES

If the edges of your granny square are wavy or uneven, it might be because of inconsistent stitch height, or too many or too few stitches.

Solution 1: Focus on making each stitch uniform in height and ensure you are working into the correct stitches and spaces along the edge.

Solution 2: Counting your stitches at the end of each round can also help maintain even edges.

LARGE HOLE IN THE CENTER

If the center of your granny square has a large, unwanted hole, it might be because the starting chain ring is too loose.

Solution 1: Take a short length of matching yarn and thread it through the posts of the first round of stitches. Gently pull on each end of the yarn to close up the hole. Tie the ends and weave them in.

Solution 2: Try using a magic ring (center ring) instead of chaining and joining, which will allow you to tighten the center more securely.

SQUARE LOSING SHAPE

If your square is starting to look more like a rectangle, or a circle, and is losing its shape, double-check your stitch placement.

Solution 1: Check that your corners have the correct number of stitches and chains, as stated in your pattern, in order to maintain the square's structure.

Solution 2: Make sure each side of the square has an equal number of stitches to keep it symmetrical.

TWISTING CENTER

Granny squares can easily twist in the center, because crochet stitches naturally lean to one side. Therefore, when you work in the round—depending on the stitch being used, along with yarn and gauge—a twisting center can be experienced.

Solution 1: When working with a single color, try turning your granny square after every round. After joining into the top of beginning ch3, turn and slip stitch into the next space to begin the round. When working with different colors for each round, turn the work before attaching the next color to any corner.

Solution 2: Whether working in a single color, or lots of colors, fasten off after each round, then re-join the yarn for next round into a different corner.

VARIATIONS ON GRANNY MOTIFS

Granny squares are a cornerstone of crochet, known for their simplicity and versatility. Each variation in this chapter retains the charm of the classic granny whilst introducing new textures, colors, and techniques. Note that no specific gauge (tension) is provided for these variations so the final size of your motif will vary depending on the yarn and hook size you choose. Always create a sample motif and adjust your yarn and hook size as needed, to achieve the preferred size and appearance.

A SNEAK PEEK AT WHAT YOU WILL FIND

- **Solid Granny Square:** A denser version of the classic, perfect for creating warm blankets and sturdy bags.
- **Daisy Flower Granny:** Add a floral motif at the center, for a delicate, nature-inspired design.
- **Circle in a Square Granny:** Start with a circle and transform it into a square, adding an interesting twist.
- **Puff Stitch Granny:** Experiment with relief stitches to add texture, depth and interest.
- **Half and Half Solid Granny:** Combine two different colors in one square for a bold, modern look that's perfect for using in quilt-inspired patterns.

SOLID GRANNY SQUARE

Now that you have the basic motifs firmly under your belt, you can try this solid, filled-in square, which uses the same techniques and stitches, in a slightly different way. This motif also works well using different colors of yarn for each round.

SOLID GRANNY SQUARE FACTS

- Instead of using granny stitch (groups of 3dc), you will work 1dc into each stitch along the sides of the motif, which creates a more solid fabric.
- As with the classic granny square, you can either start with a magic ring (see Techniques), or you can chain 5 and slip stitch into the first of these 5 ch to form a ring (see Motif 1: Starting with a Chain Ring).
- Fewer stitches are worked into the corners in order to create a flat square. This is two 2dc-groups, separated by 2 chains. These 2 chains form the corner space.

Yarn

You can use any yarn thickness to create your squares (see All About Size)

Hook

Use the hook size recommended for the yarn you are using

Extras

- Removable stitch marker
- Yarn needle

Gauge/Tension

This will depend on the yarn and hook being used. To create the same sized squares each time, use the same yarn thickness and hook size throughout.

Abbreviations

See Techniques: Abbreviations.

CHART

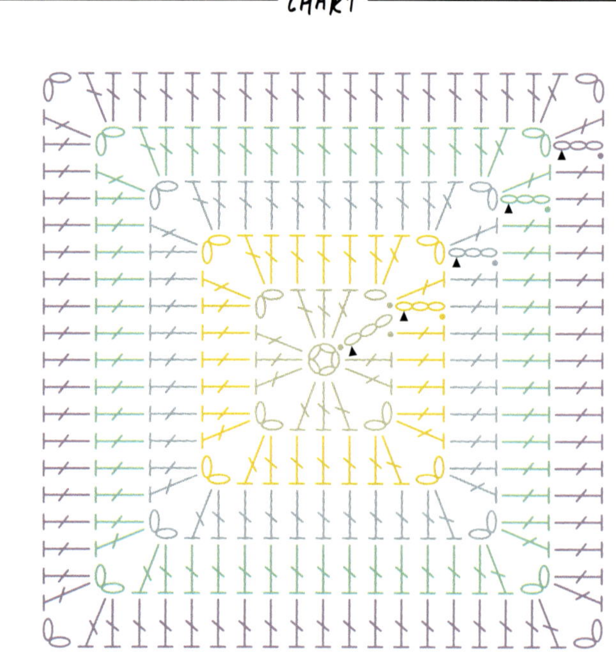

MULTI-COLORED SOLID GRANNY

PATTERN

Using first color, ch5, slst in first of these 5 ch to form a ring (see Motif 1: Starting with a Chain Ring). Alternatively, you can start with a magic ring (see Techniques).

You will now work Round 1 into the ring you have made.

Place a removable stitch marker into the center of the ring so you know where to put your hook for Round 1.

NOTE: *The first round begins with ch4. The first 3 of these 4 chains count as your first double crochet, and the fourth chain counts as your first corner space. Only 1 ch is used for the corner on this first round, because using 2 ch would make it look visibly larger than the other three corners.*

Round 1 (RS): Ch4 (counts as 1dc and corner ch-sp), [3dc in ring, ch2] 3 times, 2dc in ring, slst in third ch of beginning ch-4, slst in corner ch-sp, fasten off. (12 dc, 4 corner ch-sps)

You can join yarn to any corner to start each round.

Round 2 (RS): Join next color with slst to any corner sp, ch3 (counts as 1dc), [1dc, ch2, 2dc] in same corner sp, 1dc in each of next 3 sts, *[2dc, ch2, 2dc] in next corner sp, 1dc in each of next 3 sts; rep from * twice more, slst in third ch of beginning ch-3. (28 dc, 4 corner ch-sps)

Fasten off with invisible fasten off.

Round 3 (RS): Join next color with slst to any corner sp, ch3 (counts as 1dc), [1dc, ch2, 2dc] in same corner sp, 1dc in each dc to next corner, *[2dc, ch2, 2dc] in corner sp, 1dc in each dc to next corner; rep from * twice more, slst in third ch of beginning ch-3. (44 dc, 4 corner ch2-sps)

Fasten off with invisible fasten off.

Round 4 (RS): As Round 3. (60 dc, 4 corner ch2-sps)

Round 5 (RS): As Round 3. (76 dc, 4 corner ch2-sps)

Continue to repeat Round 3, if desired, to add more rounds to your solid granny square motif.

Fasten off with invisible fasten off, weave in ends on wrong side.

SINGLE-COLOR SOLID GRANNY SQUARE

To work your solid granny square in a single color throughout, there is no need to fasten off your yarn after every round and re-join a new color. Instead, continue with the same yarn throughout.

As with the classic granny square, after joining each round, slst into the next double crochet then slst into the corner chain space, so that your hook is in the correct place to start the next round.

This solid square is a great way to create bold projects with vivid blocks of color, and like the traditional granny square, it is quick and easy to make.

BRIGHT SQUARES BABY BLANKET

This bold blanket is perfect for adding a pop of color to a baby's room or as a thoughtful handmade gift for a new arrival. It's made up of gradient squares in rainbow colors, and you'll enjoy making it as much as gifting it. A simple border adds a neat edge, and the tassels give a fun finishing touch.

YOU WILL NEED

Yarn

Scheepjes Softfun Color Pack (60% cotton; 40% acrylic), light worsted (DK) weight, 12 x ¾oz (20g) balls, 61yd (56m) per ball

1 RAINBOW PACK:	1 PASTELS PACK:
Candy Apple (2410)	Peach (2466)
Pink (2480)	Banana (2496)
Hot Pink (2495)	Light Rose (2513)
Dark Turquoise (2511)	Rose (2514)
Deep Violet (2515)	Canary (2518)
Apple (2516)	Starfish (2620)
Violet (2519)	Arctic (2630)
Cool Blue (2603)	Green Tea (2639)
Emerald (2605)	Mint (2640)
Bumblebee (2634)	Glacial Mist (2646)
Soft Coral (2636)	Orchid (2657)
Pumpkin (2651)	Lavender (2658)

Note that not all the colors in each pack are used (see Pattern: Colors for Motifs).

Scheepjes Softfun (60% cotton; 40% acrylic), light worsted (DK) weight, 153yd (140m) per 1¾oz (50g) ball

4 x balls of Snow (2412)

Hook

US E/4 (3.5mm) crochet hook

Extras

- Removable stitch marker
- Yarn needle

Gauge/tension

Each motif measures 4¾ x 4¾in (12 x 12cm) using US E/4 (3.5mm) hook and Scheepjes Softfun.

Finished measurements

Approximately 34 x 34in (86 x 86cm)

Abbreviations

See Techniques: Abbreviations.

COLORS FOR MOTIFS

Using the Solid Granny Square motif instructions, make 36 squares, 6 of each in the following colors:

ORANGE SQUARES:

Rounds 1–3 = Peach 2466

Round 4 = Soft Coral 2636

Round 5 = Pumpkin 2651

Round 6 = Snow 2412

YELLOW SQUARES:

Rounds 1–3 = Banana 2496

Round 4 = Canary 2518

Round 5 = Bumblebee 2634

Round 6 = Snow 2412

GREEN SQUARES:

Rounds 1–3 = Green Tea 2639

Round 4 = Mint 2640

Round 5 = Emerald 2605

Round 6 = Snow 2412

BLUE SQUARES:

Rounds 1–3 Arctic 2630

Round 4 = Cool Blue 2603

Round 5 = Dark Turquoise 2511

Round 6 = Snow 2412

PURPLE SQUARES:

Rounds 1–3 = Lavender 2658

Round 4 = Orchid 2657

Round 5 = Deep Violet 2515

Round 6 = Snow 2412

PINK SQUARES:

Rounds 1–3 = Light Rose 2513

Round 4 = Rose 2514

Round 5 = Hot Pink 2495

Round 6 = Snow 2412

PATTERN BEGINS

SOLID SQUARE MOTIF

(make 36 as per Colors for Motifs)

Using chosen color as given for each round, ch5, slst in first of these 5 ch to form a ring (see Motif 1: Starting with a Chain Ring).

Place a removable stitch marker into the center of the ring so you know where to put your hook for Round 1.

Round 1 (RS): Ch4 (counts as 1dc and corner ch-sp), [3dc in ring, ch2] 3 times, 2dc in ring, slst in third ch of beginning ch-4, slst in corner ch-sp. (12 dc, 4 corner ch-sps)

Round 2 (RS): Ch3 (counts as 1dc throughout), [1dc, ch2, 2dc] in same corner sp, 1dc in each of next 3 sts, *[2dc, ch2, 2dc] in next corner sp, 1dc in each of next 3 sts; rep from * twice more, slst in third ch of beginning ch-3, slst in next dc, slst in corner ch2-sp. (28 dc, 4 corner ch-sps)

Round 3 (RS): Ch3, [1dc, ch2, 2dc] in same corner sp, 1dc in each dc to next corner, *[2dc, ch2, 2dc] in corner sp, 1dc in each dc to next corner; rep from * twice more, slst in third ch of beginning ch-3. (44 dc, 4 corner ch2-sps)

Fasten off with invisible fasten off.

Round 4 (RS): Join next color with slst to any corner sp, ch3, [1dc, ch2, 2dc] in same corner sp, 1dc in each dc to next corner, *[2dc, ch2, 2dc] in corner sp, 1dc in each dc to next corner; rep from * twice more, slst in third ch of beginning ch-3. (60 dc, 4 corner ch2-sps)

Fasten off with invisible fasten off.

Round 5 (RS): Using next color work as Round 4. (76 dc, 4 corner ch2-sps)

Round 6 (RS): Using Snow (2412) work as Round 4 but work only (1dc, ch2, 1dc) in each corner sp (84 dc, 4 corner ch2-sps)

Weave in all ends on wrong side.

JOINING

Join the squares as shown in the diagram opposite.

BORDER

The border is worked in double crochet, worked through the back loop only from Round 3 onwards.

With right side facing, join Snow (2412) with slst to any corner sp.

Round 1 (RS): Ch3 (counts as first dc throughout), [1dc, ch2, 2dc] in same corner sp, *1dc in each dc of next motif, 1dc in corner sp of this motif, dc2tog over join and first corner of next motif, **1dc in each dc of motif and 1dc in corner sp of motif, dc2tog over join and corner sp of next motif; rep from ** across all motifs to next corner of full blanket, [2dc, ch2, 2dc] in corner of blanket; rep from * all around blanket, ending with slst in third ch of beginning ch-3, slst in next dc, slst in corner ch-sp. (140 dc along each side of blanket, 4 ch2-sps)

Round 2 (RS): Ch3, [1dc, ch2, 2dc] in same corner sp, 1dc in each dc to next corner, *[2dc, ch2, 2dc] in corner of blanket, 1dc in each dc to next corner; rep from * to end, slst in third ch of beginning ch-3. (144 dc along each side of blanket, 4 ch2-sps)

Fasten off with invisible fasten off.

Round 3 (RS): Join Apple (2516) with slst to any corner sp, ch3 (counts as first dc), [1dc, ch2, 2dc] in same corner sp, 1dcBLO in each dc to next corner, *[2dc, ch2, 2dc] in corner of blanket, 1dcBLO in each dc to next corner; rep from * to end, slst in third ch of beginning ch-3. (148 dc along each side of blanket, 4 ch2-sps)

Fasten off with invisible fasten off.

Round 4 (RS): Using Snow (2412), rep Round 3. (152 dc along each side of blanket, 4 ch2-sps)

Fasten off with invisible fasten off.

Round 4 (RS): Using Snow (2412), rep Round 3. (152 dc along each side of blanket, 4 ch2-sps)

Fasten off with invisible fasten off.

Round 5 (RS): Using Violet (2519), rep Round 3. (156 dc along each side of blanket, 4 ch2-sps)

Fasten off with invisible fasten off.

Round 6 (RS): Using Snow (2412), rep Round 3. (160 dc along each side of blanket, 4 ch2-sps)

Fasten off.

Round 7 (RS): Using Pink (2480), rep Round 3. (164 dc along each side of blanket, 4 ch2-sps)

Fasten off with invisible fasten off, weave in all ends on wrong side.

TASSELS

Make 4 tassels using Apple (2516) and 4 tassels using Violet (2519) (see Techniques: Making a Tassel).

Attach 2 tassels (one in each color) to the blanket corners, using the yarn ends from the top of the tassels.

FINISHING

Pin flat, steam block and leave to dry completely.

JOINING

Using whip stitch (see Joining Techniques: Whip Stitch/Oversewing), join the squares in the order as shown in the diagram below. First join the squares together to form strips, then whip stitch the strips together.

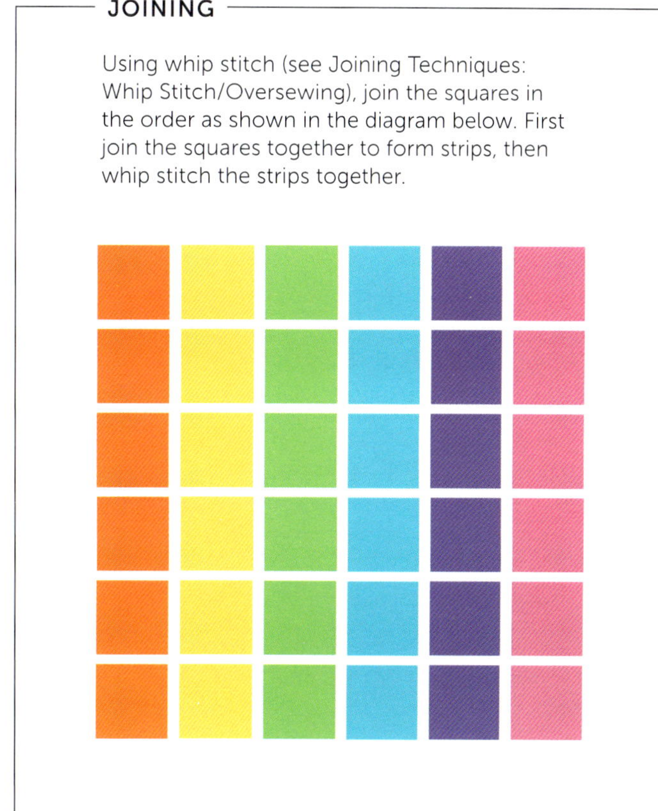

DAISY FLOWER GRANNY

This motif uses a treble crochet cluster stitch to create a flower effect in the center. The initial flower is then turned into a square by creating four corner stitches.

DAISY FLOWER GRANNY FACTS

- The motif is a simple variation of the multi-color classic granny square, incorporating a central floral motif, which transitions into a square by adding corner stitches. Whilst it might look intricate, the motif is accessible to beginners who are comfortable with basic crochet stitches.
- As with the classic granny square, you can either start with a magic ring (see Techniques), or you can chain 5 and slip stitch into the first of these 5 ch to form a ring (see Motif 1: Starting with a Chain Ring).

SPECIAL STITCH

- **3 treble crochet cluster (3tr-CL):** *Yarn over twice, insert hook in stitch, yarn over, pull up a loop, [yarn over, pull through 2 loops] twice* (2 loops on hook); rep from * to * twice more (4 loops on hook), yarn over, pull through 4 loops to finish.

Yarn

You can use any yarn thickness to create your squares (see All About Size)

Hook

Use the hook size recommended for the yarn you are using

Extras

- Removable stitch marker
- Yarn needle

Gauge/Tension

This will depend on the yarn and hook being used. To create the same sized squares each time, use the same yarn thickness and hook size throughout.

Abbreviations

See Techniques: Abbreviations.

CHART

PATTERN

Using Yellow, ch5, slst in first of these 5 ch to form a ring (see Motif 1: Starting with a Chain Ring). Alternatively, you can start with a magic ring (see Techniques).

You will now work Round 1 into the ring you have made.

Place a removable stitch marker into the center of the ring so you know where to put your hook for Round 1.

Round 1 (RS): Ch3 (counts as 1dc), 11dc in ring, slst in third ch of beginning ch-3. (12 dc)

Fasten off with invisible fasten off.

Round 2 (RS): Join White or Cream with slst to any st, ch1 (does not count as a st), 3tr-CL in same st, ch2, [3tr-CL in next st, ch2] 11 times more, skip the first 3tr-CL and slst in the next ch2-sp. (12 tr-CL, 12 ch2-sps)

Fasten off with invisible fasten off.

Round 3 (RS): Join Green with slst to any ch2-sp, ch4 (counts as 1tr), [2tr, ch2, 3tr] in same ch-2 sp, ch1, [3dc in next ch2-sp, ch1] twice, *[3tr, ch2, 3tr] in next ch2-sp, ch1, [3dc in next ch2-sp, ch1] twice; rep from * twice more, slst in fourth ch of beginning ch-4, slst in each of next 2 tr and slst in corner ch2-sp. (8 3dc-groups, 8 3tr-groups, 12 ch1-sps, 4 corner ch2-sps)

Round 4 (RS): Ch3 (counts as 1dc), [2dc, ch2, 3dc] in same corner sp, ch1, [3dc in next ch1-sp, ch1] to next corner sp, *[3dc, ch2, 3dc] in corner sp, ch1, [3dc in next ch1-sp, ch1] to next corner sp; rep from * twice more, slst in third ch of beginning ch-3. (5 3dc-groups along each side, four corner ch2-sps)

To add more rounds to your daisy flower motif you can continue to rep Round 4, but to get to the right starting position for each round work a slst in each of next 2 dc and in the corner ch2-sp.

Fasten off, weave in all ends on wrong side.

DAISY GARDEN SNUG COWL

We're still keeping things really simple with this pretty cowl. This project uses daisy square motifs that are joined together by whip stitch to create a stylish accessory that will keep those chills at bay. Using a gradient yarn helps to create a beautiful, variegated effect, where each motif is slightly different than the last, which makes it fun and interesting to make, too.

YOU WILL NEED

Yarn

Scheepjes Secret Garden (20% silk; 20% cotton; 60% polyester), light worsted (DK) weight, 101yd (93m) per 1¾oz (50g) ball

Color 1: 1 ball of Summer House (707)

Color 2: 1 ball of Rose Arch (708)

Color 3: 2 balls of Herb Garden (702)

Hook

US E/4 (3.5mm) crochet hook

Extras

- Removable stitch marker
- Yarn needle

Gauge/tension

Each motif measures 3 x 3in (7.6 x 7.6cm) using US E/4 (3.5mm) hook and Scheepjes Secret Garden.

Finished measurements

27 x 10in (68.5 x 25.5cm)

Abbreviations

See Techniques: Abbreviations.

Special stitch

3 treble crochet cluster (3tr-CL): *Yarn over twice, insert hook in stitch, yarn over, pull up a loop, [yarn over, pull through 2 loops] twice* (2 loops on hook); rep from * to * twice more (4 loops on hook), yarn over, pull through 4 loops to finish.

PATTERN NOTES

This cowl is made up of 27 small daisy flower granny motifs.

14 are made using Color 1 as center and Color 2 for Round 2;

13 are made using Color 2 as center and Color 1 for Round 2.

The motifs are worked individually and then joined and seamed on wrong side to form a tube. An edging is added to complete the cowl. The square motifs are based on the daisy flower granny motif using Rounds 1 to 3 only.

PATTERN BEGINS

DAISY FLOWER MOTIF

(make 27 in colors as given in Pattern Notes)

Using Color 1, ch5, slst in first of these 5 ch to form a ring (see Motif 1: Starting with a Chain Ring). Alternatively, you can start with a magic ring (see Techniques).

You will now work Round 1 into the ring you have made.

Place a removable stitch marker into the center of the ring so you know where to put your hook for Round 1.

Round 1 (RS): Ch3 (counts as 1dc), 11dc in ring, slst in third ch of beginning ch-3. (12 dc)

Fasten off with invisible fasten off.

Round 2 (RS): Join Color 2 with slst to any st, ch1 (does not count as a st), 3tr-CL in same st, ch2, [3tr-CL in next st, ch2] 11 times more, skip the first 3tr-CL and slst in the next ch2-sp. (12 tr-CL and 12 ch2-sps)

Fasten off.

Round 3 (RS): Join Color 3 with slst to any ch2-sp, ch4 (counts as 1tr), [2tr, ch2, 3tr] in same ch-2 sp, ch1, [3dc in next ch2-sp, ch1] twice, *[3tr, ch2, 3tr] in next ch2-sp, ch1, [3dc in next ch2-sp, ch1] twice; rep from * twice more, slst in fourth ch of beginning ch-4. (8 3dc-groups, 8 3tr-groups, 12 ch1-sps, 4 corner ch2-sps)

Fasten off with invisible fasten off, weave in all ends on wrong side.

JOINING

Join the squares as shown in the diagram on the right.

EDGING

Work along top and bottom edges only.

With right side facing, join Color 3 with slst to any st.

Round 1 (RS): Ch1 (does not count as a st), 1sc in same st at base of beginning ch-1, 1sc in each st to end and 1hdc in each joining seam, slst in first sc.

Fasten off with invisible fasten off.

FINISHING

Spray one side of cowl with cold water until damp. Pin flat to a blocking board and leave to dry. Turn cowl over and repeat on opposite side.

JOINING

Lay out the squares in a pleasing order in 3 rows of 9 squares. Using Color 3, join the squares using whip stitch (see Joining Techniques: Whip Stitch/Oversewing), for a flat, seamless finish. Join the squares horizontally across the rows then join the vertical seams. Join the ends to form a tube. Fasten off and weave in all ends on the wrong side.

CIRCLE IN A SQUARE GRANNY

This motif begins with double crochet stitches to create the circular motif center, which is worked in Rounds 1 and 2. In Round 3 you begin to crochet a square to frame the circle, by working the four corners.

CIRCLE IN A SQUARE GRANNY FACTS

- When transitioning from the circle to the square, you'll work into the back bumps of the stitches from the final round of the circle. This helps create a crisp, clean edge to the center circle.
- The back bump sits behind the top two loops of the stitch.
- As with the classic granny square, you can either start with a magic ring (see Techniques), or you can chain 5 and slip stitch into the first of these 5 ch to form a ring (see Motif 1: Starting with a Chain Ring).

Yarn

You can use any yarn thickness to create your squares (see All About Size)

Hook

Use the hook size recommended for the yarn you are using

Extras

- Removable stitch marker
- Yarn needle

Gauge/Tension

This will depend on the yarn and hook being used. To create the same sized squares each time, use the same yarn thickness and hook size throughout.

Abbreviations

See Techniques: Abbreviations.

CHART

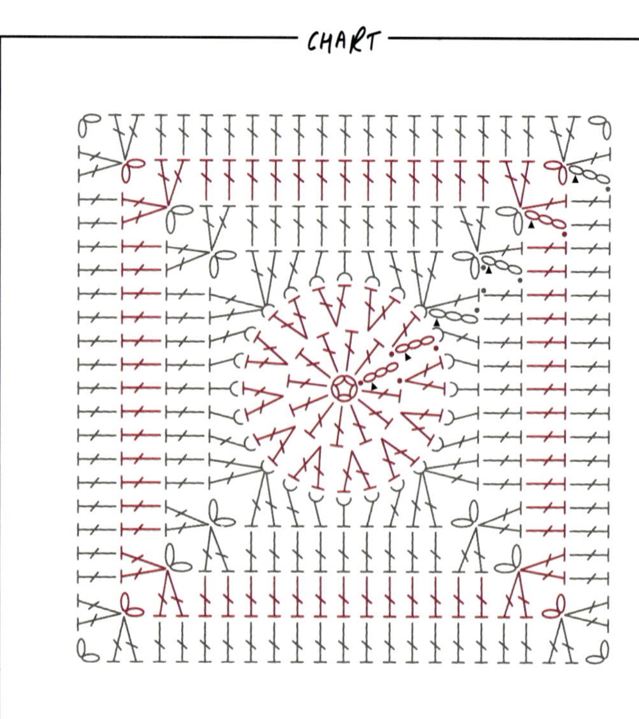

PATTERN

Using Contrast Color, ch5, slst in first of these 5 ch to form a ring (see Motif 1: Starting with a Chain Ring). Alternatively, you can start with a magic ring (see Techniques).

You will now work Round 1 into the ring you have made.

Place a removable stitch marker into the center of the ring so you know where to put your hook for Round 1.

Round 1 (RS): Ch3 (counts as 1dc throughout), 11dc in ring, slst in third ch of beginning ch-3, slst in space before next dc. (12 dc)

Round 2 (RS): Ch3, 1dc in same sp, 2dc in each sp between dc sts, slst in third ch of beginning ch-3. (24 dc)

Fasten off with invisible fasten off.

Join Main Color in back bump (bb) of any stitch (see Techniques). This is the small strand of yarn sitting behind the top of the stitch and leaves the top of the stitch completely visible to create a perfect circle shape.

Round 3 (RS): Ch3, [1dc, ch2, 2dc] in bb of same st, 1dc in bb of next st, 1hdc in bb of next 3 sts, 1dc in bb of next st, *[2dc, ch2, 2dc] in bb of next st, 1dc in bb of next st, 1hdc in bb of next 3 sts, 1dc in bb of next st; rep from * twice more, slst in third ch of beginning ch-3, slst in next dc, slst in corner ch2-sp. (12 hdc, 24 dc, 4 ch2-sps)

Round 4 (RS): Ch3, [1dc, ch2, 2dc] in same corner sp, 1dc in each st to next corner, *[2dc, ch2, 2dc] in corner sp, 1dc in each st to next corner; rep from * twice more, slst in third ch of beginning ch-3. (52 dc, 4 ch2-sps)

Fasten off with invisible fasten off.

Round 5 (RS): Join Contrast Color to any corner ch-sp, work as Round 4. (68 dc, 4 ch2-sps)

Fasten off with invisible fasten off.

Round 6 (RS): Join Main Color to any corner ch-sp, work as Round 4. (84 dc, 4 ch2-sps)

Fasten off with invisible fasten off, weave in ends on wrong side.

DOTTY DAYS TOTE BAG

This statement accessory has nine circle in a square motifs on each side, joined to create a stylish and functional bag to carry daily essentials. Each square begins with a vibrant, colorful circle and transitions into a solid granny square, showcasing a blend of classic and modern crochet techniques. Wooden handles add a touch of rustic charm, making this bag a perfect accessory for any occasion.

YOU WILL NEED

Yarn

Scheepjes Terrazzo (70% wool; 30% viscose), light worsted (DK) weight, 191yd (175m) per 1¾oz (50g) ball

Main Color: 2 balls of Pergamena (745)

CONTRAST COLORS:

Color 1: 1 ball of Limone (702)

Color 2: 1 ball of Lampone (721)

Color 3: 1 ball of Fontana (735)

Color 4: 1 ball of Oliva (707)

Hook

US E/4 (3.5mm) crochet hook

Extras

- Removable stitch marker
- Yarn needle
- Pair of D-shaped wooden bag handles, approximately 6¾in (17cm) wide
- Optional lining fabric 28½ x 14¼in (72 x 36cm), sewing needle and thread

Gauge/tension

Each motif measures 4½ x 4½in (11 x 11cm) using US E/4 (3.5mm) hook and Scheepjes Terrazzo.

Finished measurements

Approximately 13½ x 13½in (34 x 34cm)

Abbreviations

See Techniques: Abbreviations.

PATTERN NOTES

This bag is made up of individual motifs that are crocheted together with a single crochet seam.

It's the perfect project for using up oddments of light worsted (DK) yarn, or you can use the yarn specified.

Gauge is not critical for this project.

PATTERN BEGINS

CIRCLE IN A SQUARE MOTIF

(make 18, 4 each with Color 1, Color 3, and Color 4 centers, 6 with Color 2 center)

Using chosen color for center, ch5, slst in first of these 5 ch to form a ring (see Motif 1: Starting with a Chain Ring). Alternatively, you can start with a magic ring (see Techniques).

You will now work Round 1 into the ring you have made.

Place a removable stitch marker into the center of the ring so you know where to put your hook for Round 1.

Round 1 (RS): Ch3 (counts as 1dc), 11dc in ring, slst in third ch of beginning ch-3, slst in space before next dc. (12 dc)

Round 2 (RS): Ch3 (counts as 1dc), 1dc in same sp, 2dc in each sp between dc stitches, slst in third ch of beginning ch-3. (24 dc)

Fasten off with invisible fasten off.

Join Main Color in back bump (bb) of any stitch (see Techniques).

Round 3 (RS): Ch3 (counts as 1dc), [1dc, ch2, 2dc] in same st, 1dc in bb of next st, 1hdc in bb of next 3 sts, 1dc in bb of next st, *[2dc, ch2, 2dc] in bb of next st, 1dc in bb of next st, 1hdc in bb of next 3 sts, 1dc in bb of next st; rep from * twice more, slst in third ch of beginning ch-3, slst in next dc, slst in corner ch2-sp. (12 hdc, 24 dc, 4 ch2-sps)

Round 4 (RS): Ch3 (counts as 1dc), [1dc, ch2, 2dc] in same corner sp, 1dc in each st to next corner, *[2dc, ch2, 2dc] in corner sp, 1dc in each st to next corner; rep from * twice more, slst in third ch of beginning ch-3. (52 dc, 4 ch2-sps)

Fasten off with invisible fasten off.

Round 5 (RS): Join same color as center to any corner ch-sp. Work as Round 4. (68 dc, 4 ch2-sps)

Fasten off with invisible fasten off.

Join Main Color to any corner ch-sp.

Round 6 (RS): As Round 4. (84 dc, 4 ch2-sps)

Fasten off with invisible fasten off, weave in ends on wrong side.

JOINING

Join the squares as shown in the diagram on the right.

BORDER

The border is worked on both sides the same.

With right side facing, and with Main Color, join with slst to any corner sp of the large square.

Round 1 (RS): Ch1 (does not count as a st), *[1sc, ch2, 1sc] in corner sp, work sc across the edge stitches of first side, working 1sc in each st, 1sc in corner sps of each motif and 1hdc in each joining seam; rep from * 3 times more across each side of square, slst in first sc, slst in corner sp and fasten off. (71 sts along each side; 284 sts in total and 4 corner ch2-sps)

Join any Contrast Color to a corner ch2-sp.

Round 2 (RS): Ch1 (does not count as a st), *[1sc, ch2, 1sc] in corner, 1sc in each st to next corner; rep from * to end, slst in first sc, slst in corner sp and fasten off. (73 sts along each side; 292 sts in total and 4 corner ch2-sps)

Join Main Color to any corner ch2-sp.

Round 3 (RS): Repeat Round 2. (75 sts along each side; 300 sts in total and 4 corner ch2-sps)

Fasten off, weave in ends on wrong side.

JOINING

Lay out the squares in a pleasing order in 3 rows of 3 squares. Use the diagram as a guide to placement. Using the Main Color, join the squares using a single crochet seam or, if preferred, you can join with a sewn whip stitch seam (see Joining Techniques). Weave in all ends.

FINISHING

Spray front and back of bag with cold water until damp. Pin flat and leave to dry (see Techniques: Blocking).

JOINING FRONT AND BACK

Place wrong sides of bag together and join three sides only, by working though both pieces as follows: join Main Color with slst through both pieces of any corner. Ch1, work 1sc in same corner sp, then 1sc in each st to next corner sp, 3sc in corner sp, 1sc in each st to next corner, 3sc in corner, 1sc in each st to next corner sp, 1sc in corner sp.

Fasten off, weave in ends on wrong side and trim.

TOP EDGE

For this project you will work a Moss Stitch Border around the top edge of the bag.

See Borders: Moss Stitch Border for an example chart of this border.

Round 1 (RS): Join Main Color with slst through any joining side seam, ch1 (does not count as a stitch), work 1sc in same place, [ch1, skip next st, 1sc in next st] all around, to last st, ch1, skip last st, slst in first sc. (152 sts)

Round 2 (RS): Slst in next ch1-sp, ch1 (does not count as a stitch), work 1sc in same sp, [ch1, skip next st, 1sc in next ch1-sp] all around, to last st, ch1, skip last st, slst in first sc.

Fasten off, weave in ends on wrong side.

LINING

If desired, you can line your bag for extra support, as follows: using the bag as a template, draw around it onto paper. Cut out and then use this template to cut two squares of fabric, adding an extra ¼in (0.5cm) all around for seams.

With right sides of the fabric together, join around three sides only, with a ¼in (0.5cm) seam allowance.

Fold over the top edge by ¾in (1cm) to the wrong side and press flat. Machine stitch the hem, if desired.

Slide the fabric lining into the crochet bag with wrong sides together and sew the lining to inside top border of bag, using small stitches, and sewing along the folded line of the fabric.

HANDLES

On each side of the bag, count three stitches away from each side of center square and place a stitch marker in each stitch, to mark the position to join the handle.

Using the Main Color, make a slip knot on the hook. With wrong side facing, join the Main Color with a slst to the marked stitch on the right. Place the base of handle along the working edge and behind the working yarn.

Yarn over hook and pull a loop through, making sure the yarn is now around the handle base, lengthen the stitch slightly to bring it in line with the top of the handle base, yarn over and pull through the loops on the hook to complete first single crochet.

Continue working single crochet through every stitch along the top of the motif, inserting the hook in the stitch and under the base of the wooden handle to trap it into the stitches, and lengthening the stitch when working each single crochet.

When you reach the opposite side of the handle at the marked stitch, fasten off.

Weave in all ends and trim.

Repeat for opposite side.

PUFF STITCH GRANNY

This motif introduces puff stitch for the center and the corners of the square, to add a simple raised pattern for extra interest.

PUFF STITCH GRANNY FACTS

- Puff stitch is classed as a relief stitch, and it resembles a bobble. It stands out visibly with its beautiful texture, and is also very tactile.
- It works well in a single color throughout.

SPECIAL STITCH

- **puff-st (puff stitch):** *Yarn over, insert hook in st or sp indicated, yarn over and pull loop through* (3 loops on hook); rep from * to * 3 times more into same st or sp (9 loops on hook), yarn over and carefully pull through all 9 loops, and finally, ch1 to close the puff stitch.

Important note: The closing ch1 forms the top of the puff stitch and does not form part of the chains that follow.

Yarn

You can use any yarn thickness to create your squares (see All About Size)

Hook

Use the hook size recommended for the yarn you are using

Extras

- Removable stitch marker
- Yarn needle

Gauge/Tension

This will depend on the yarn and hook being used. To create the same sized squares each time, use the same yarn thickness and hook size throughout.

Abbreviations

See Techniques: Abbreviations.

CHART

PATTERN

Using chosen color, ch5, slst in first of these 5 ch to form a ring (see Motif 1: Starting with a Chain Ring). Alternatively, you can start with a magic ring (see Techniques).

You will now work Round 1 into the ring you have made.

Place a removable stitch marker into the center of the ring so you know where to put your hook for Round 1.

Round 1 (RS): [Puff-st in ring, ch2] 4 times, slst in top of first puff-st, slst in corner ch2-sp. (4 puff-sts, 4 corner ch2-sps)

Round 2 (RS): [Puff-st, ch2, puff-st] in same corner sp, ch1, *[puff-st, ch2, puff-st] in next corner sp, ch1; rep from * twice more, slst in top of first puff-st, slst in corner sp. (8 puff-sts, 4 corner ch2-sps, 4 ch1-sps)

Round 3 (RS): [Puff-st, ch2, puff-st] in same corner sp, ch1, 3dc in next ch1-sp, ch1, *[puff-st, ch2, puff-st] in next corner sp, ch1, 3dc in next ch1-sp, ch1; rep from * twice more, slst in top of first puff-st, slst in corner ch2-sp. (8 puff-sts, 4 3dc-groups, 4 corner ch2-sps, 8 ch1-sps)

Round 4 (RS): [Puff-st, ch2, puff-st] in same corner sp, ch1, [3dc in next ch1-sp, ch1] to next corner, *[puff-st, ch2, puff-st] in next corner sp, ch1, [3dc in next ch1-sp, ch1] to next corner; rep from * twice more, slst in top of first puff-st, slst in corner ch2-sp. (8 puff-sts, 8 3dc-groups, 4 corner ch2-sps, 12 ch1-sps)

Round 5 (RS): As Round 4 but fasten off after joining round with slst. (8 puff-sts, 12 3dc-groups, 4 corner ch2-sps, 16 ch1-sps)

To make your square larger, do not fasten off after Round 5—instead slst in the corner ch2-sp then continue to repeat Round 4 to add more rounds.

Fasten off, weave in ends on wrong side.

CUTE AND COZY TASSELED SCARF

This warm and colorful accessory is based on the puff stitch motif, with each motif worked in a solid color and edged with the main color. The squares are joined with a whip stitch seam for a simple finish, with an edging for a neat finish and tassels for the final flourish.

YOU WILL NEED

Yarn

Scheepjes Scrumptious (50% recycled polyester; 50% acrylic), light worsted (DK) weight, 328yd (300m) per 3½oz (100g) ball

Main Color: 2 balls of Cosmic Cupcake (366)

Color 1: ⅓ ball of Blue Glazed Doughnut (314)

Color 2: ⅓ ball of Orange Cheesecake (332)

Color 3: ⅓ ball of Custard Pie (341)

Color 4: ⅓ ball of Buttercream Icing (302)

Color 5: ⅓ ball of Rainforest Cake (349)

Color 6: ⅓ ball of Strawberry Shortcake (309)

Color 7: ⅓ ball of Keylime Pie (337)

Color 8: ⅓ ball of Shamrock Shortbread (350)

Color 9: ⅓ ball of Blackberry Honey Gelato (312)

Color 10: ⅓ ball of Honeycomb Crunch (310)

Hook

US G/6 (4mm) crochet hook

Extras

- Removable stitch marker
- Yarn needle
- Cardboard for tassel

Gauge/tension

Each motif measures 4½ x 4½in (11 x 11cm) using US G/6 (4mm) hook and Scheepjes Scrumptious.

Finished measurements

52¾ x 18in (134 x 46cm)

Abbreviations

See Techniques: Abbreviations.

Special stitch

puff-st (puff stitch): *Yarn over, insert hook in st or sp indicated, yarn over and pull loop through* (3 loops on hook); rep from * to * 3 times more into same st or sp (9 loops on hook), yarn over and carefully pull through all 9 loops, finally ch1 to close the puff stitch.

Important note: This ch1 forms the top of the puff stitch and does not form part of the chains that follow.

PATTERN NOTES

This scarf is made up of individual puff stitch motifs that are sewn together with a whip stitch seam.

You need around 1oz (30g) each of Colors 1–10 so it's the perfect project for using up oddments of light worsted (DK) yarn, or you can use the yarn specified.

Gauge is not critical for this project.

PATTERN BEGINS

PUFF STITCH MOTIF

(make 45, 7 in Color 4, 5 each in Colors 3 and 7, 4 each in Colors 1, 2, 5, 6. 8, 9, 10)

Using chosen color, ch5, slst in first of these 5 ch to form a ring (see Motif 1: Starting with a Chain Ring). Alternatively, you can start with a magic ring (see Techniques).

You will now work Round 1 into the ring you have made.

Place a removable stitch marker into the center of the ring so you know where to put your hook for Round 1.

Round 1 (RS): [Puff-st in ring, ch2] 4 times, slst in top of first puff-st, slst in corner ch2-sp. (4 puff-sts and 4 corner ch2-sps)

Round 2 (RS): [Puff-st, ch2, puff-st] in same corner sp, ch1, *[puff-st, ch2, puff-st] in next corner sp, ch1; rep from * twice more, slst in top of first puff-st, slst in corner sp. (8 puff-sts, 4 corner ch2-sps, 4 ch1-sps)

Round 3 (RS): [Puff-st, ch2, puff-st] in same corner sp, ch1, 3dc in next ch1-sp, ch1, *[puff-st, ch2, puff-st] in next corner sp, ch1, 3dc in next ch1-sp, ch1; rep from * twice more, slst in top of first puff-st, slst in corner ch2-sp. (8 puff-sts, 12 dc, 4 corner ch2-sps, 8 ch1-sps)

Round 4 (RS): [Puff-st, ch2, puff-st] in same corner sp, ch1, [3dc in next ch1-sp, ch1] to next corner, *[puff-st, ch2, puff-st] in next corner sp, ch1, [3tr in next ch1-sp, ch1] to next corner; rep from * twice more, slst in top of first puff-st, slst in corner ch2-sp. (8 puff-sts, 4 3dc-groups, 4 corner ch2-sps, 12 ch1-sps)

Round 5 (RS): As Round 4. (8 puff-sts 12 3dc-groups, 4 corner ch2-sps, 16 ch1-sps)

Fasten off.

Round 6 (RS): [Puff-st, ch2, puff-st] in same corner sp, 1dc in each st and ch1-sp to next corner, *[puff-st, ch2, puff-st] in next corner sp, 1dc in each st and ch1-sp to next corner; rep from * twice more, slst in top of first puff-st, slst in corner ch2-sp. (8 puff-sts, 60 dc, 4 corner ch2-sps)

Fasten off.

JOINING

Join the squares as shown in the diagram on the right.

BORDER

With right side facing, join Main Color with slst to any corner of scarf.

Round 1 (RS): Ch1 (does not count as a st throughout), *[2sc, ch2, 2sc] in corner ch-sp, 1sc in every st to ch-sp before next joining seam, **2sc in ch-sp, 1sc in joining seam, 2sc in ch-sp of next motif, 1sc in every st of next motif to ch-sp before next joining seam; rep from ** until you reach next corner ch-sp of scarf*; then rep from * to * three times more, slst in first sc, slst in next sc, slst into corner ch-sp. (788 sts, 4 corner ch2-sps)

Round 2 (RS): Ch1, *[1sc, ch2, 1sc] in same corner sp, ch1, skip 1 st, [1sc in next st, ch1, skip 1 st] to next corner sp, *[1sc, ch2, 1sc] in corner sp, ch1, skip 1 st [1sc in next st, ch1, skip 1 st] to next corner sp; rep from * to end, slst in first sc, slst into corner ch-sp. (796 sts, 4 corner ch2-sps)

Round 3 (RS): Ch1, *3sc in corner ch-sp, 2sc in each ch1-sp to next corner; rep from * 3 times more, slst in first sc. (808 sts)

Fasten off with invisible fasten off.

FINISHING

Spray scarf with cold water until damp. Pin flat to a blocking board and leave to dry (see Techniques: Blocking).

JOINING

Lay out the squares in a pleasing order in 3 rows of 15 squares as shown in the diagram below. Using the Main Color, join the squares using whip stitch, for a flat, seamless finish or, if preferred, you can join with a slip stitch or single crochet seam (see Joining Techniques). Weave in all ends.

TASSELS

Make 8 tassels (see Techniques: Making a Tassel), using any colors of choice, and attach 4 tassels, evenly spaced, to short edges, in corners and in line with seams.

HALF AND HALF SOLID GRANNY

This motif is classed as advanced, because the yarn color is changed part-way along each round. However, once you have mastered the technique, you can create so many different patterns with this half and half solid granny square.

HALF AND HALF SOLID GRANNY FACTS

- This motif is ideal for creating eye-catching blankets, throws, and cushion covers with bold color-blocked patterns.
- The clear color division offers a unique geometric design suitable for many types of crochet projects, and it is also the perfect motif for quilt-inspired designs.

Yarn

You can use any yarn thickness to create your squares (see All About Size)

Hook

Use the hook size recommended for the yarn you are using

Extras

- Removable stitch marker
- Yarn needle

Gauge/Tension

This will depend on the yarn and hook being used. To create the same sized squares each time, use the same yarn thickness and hook size throughout.

Abbreviations

See Techniques: Abbreviations.

CHART

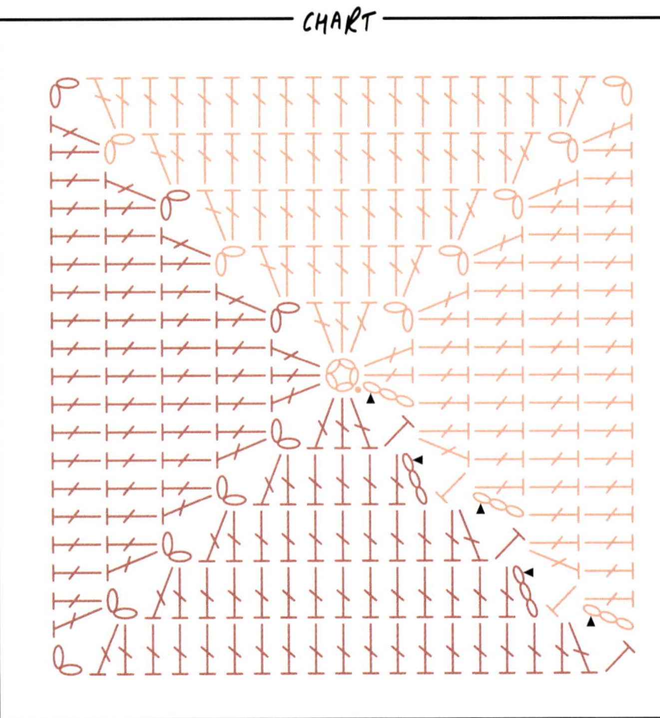

PATTERN

Using Color 1, ch5, slst in first of these 5 ch to form a ring (see Motif 1: Starting with a Chain Ring). Alternatively, you can start with a magic ring (see Techniques).

You will now work Round 1 into the ring you have made.

Place a removable stitch marker into the center of the ring so you know where to put your hook for Round 1.

Round 1 (RS): Ch3 (counts as 1dc), 2dc in ring, ch2, 3dc in ring, changing to Color 2 on last yoh of last dc, (let go of Color 1 and leave it at this point), ch2, 3dc in ring, ch2, 3dc in ring, hdc in top of the third ch of beginning ch-3, turn. (12 dc, 4 corner ch2-spaces)

Round 2 (WS): First half: Using Color 2, ch3 (counts as 1dc), 1dc in same sp, 1dc in each st to next corner sp, [2dc, ch2, 2dc] in corner sp, 1dc in each st to next corner sp, 1dc in corner, lift Color 1 and lay it across corner to crochet over it, work 1dc in corner sp, changing to Color 1 on last yoh of last dc. Second half: Using Color 1, ch2, 2dc in corner sp, 1dc in each st to next corner sp, [2dc, ch2, 2dc] in corner sp, 1dc in each st to next corner sp, 2dc in corner sp, hdc in third ch of beginning ch-3, turn. (28 dc, 4 ch2-sps)

Round 3 (RS): First half: Using Color 1, ch3 (counts as 1dc), 1dc in same sp, 1dc in each st to next corner sp, [2dc, ch2, 2dc] in corner sp, 1dc in each st to next corner ch2-sp, 1dc in corner sp, lift Color 2 and lay it across corner to crochet over it, work 1dc in corner, changing to Color 2 on last yoh of last dc. Second half: Using Color 2, ch2, 2dc in corner sp, 1dc in each st to next corner sp, [2dc, ch2, 2dc] in corner sp, 1dc in each st to next corner sp, 2dc in corner sp, hdc in third ch of beginning ch-3. (44 dc, 4 ch2-sps)

Repeat Rounds 2 and 3 until your square is the required size.

Fasten off, weave in ends on wrong side.

RADIANT STAR CUSHION

This cushion features a unique star shape, created from half and half solid granny squares, providing a modern twist to a traditional pattern. This star design is a popular, traditional quilt design and uses three different colors of yarn to create a stand-out home accessory. You only need to make the front of the cushion, which is then stitched to the front of a fabric cushion cover.

YOU WILL NEED

Yarn

Scheepjes Catona (100% cotton), fingering (4ply) weight, 136yd (125m) per 1¾oz (50g) ball

1 ball of Icy Pink (246)

1 ball of Bluebird (247)

1 ball of Bridal White (105)

Hook

US E/4 (3.5mm) crochet hook

Extras

- Removable stitch marker
- Yarn needle
- 12 x 12in (30 x 30cm) cushion in a light color (white or cream)
- Sewing needle and matching thread

Gauge/tension

Each motif measures approximately 2½ x 2½in (6.25 x 6.25cm) using US E/4 (3.5mm) hook and Scheepjes Catona.

Finished measurements

To fit a cushion that measures 12 x 12in (30 x 30cm)

Abbreviations

See Techniques: Abbreviations.

COLORS FOR HALF AND HALF MOTIFS

Four in Icy Pink for Color 1 and Bluebird for Color 2.

Eight in Bluebird for Color 1 and Bridal White for Color 2.

COLOR FOR PLAIN SOLID MOTIFS

Four in Bridal White.

PATTERN BEGINS

HALF AND HALF MOTIFS

(make 12 as listed in Colors for Half and Half Motifs)

Using Color 1, ch5, slst in first of these 5 ch to form a ring (see Motif 1: Starting with a Chain Ring). Alternatively, you can start with a magic ring (see Techniques).

You will now work Round 1 into the ring you have made.

Place a removable stitch marker into the center of the ring so you know where to put your hook for Round 1.

Round 1 (RS): Ch3 (counts as 1dc throughout), 2dc in ring, ch2, 3dc in ring, changing to Color 2 on last yoh of last dc (let go of Color 1 and leave it at this point), ch2, [3dc in ring, ch2] twice, hdc in top of the third ch of beginning ch-3, turn. (12 dc and 4 corner ch2-spaces)

Round 2 (WS): First half: Using Color 2, slst in next corner ch2-sp, ch3 (counts as 1dc), 1dc in same sp, 1dc in each st to next corner ch2-sp, [2dc, ch2, 2dc] in corner ch-sp, 1dc in each st to next corner ch2-sp, 1dc in corner, lift Color 1 and lay it across corner to crochet over it, work 1dc into corner, changing to Color 1 on last yoh of last dc. Second half: Ch2, 2dc in corner sp, 1dc in each st to next corner ch2-sp, [2dc, ch2, 2dc] in corner ch-sp, 1dc in each st to next corner ch2-sp, 2dc in corner, hdc in third ch of beginning ch-3, turn.

Round 3 (RS): First half: Using Color 1, ch3 (counts as 1dc), 1dc in same sp, 1dc in each st to next corner ch2-sp, [2dc, ch2, 2dc] in corner sp, 1dc in each st to next corner ch2-sp, 1dc in corner sp, lift Color 2 and lay it across corner to crochet over it, work 1dc into corner, changing to Color 2 on last yoh of last dc. Second half: Ch2, 2dc in corner sp, 1dc in each st to next corner ch2-sp, [2dc, ch2, 2dc] in corner ch-sp, 1dc in each st to next corner ch2-sp, 2dc in corner, hdc in third ch of beginning ch-3. (44 dc and 4 corner ch2-sps)

Fasten off, weave in ends on wrong side.

PLAIN COLOR SOLID MOTIFS

(make 4)

Using Bridal White, ch5, slst in first of these 5 ch to form a ring (see Motif 1: Starting with a Chain Ring). Alternatively, you can start with a magic ring (see Techniques).

You will now work Round 1 into the ring you have made.

Place a removable stitch marker into the center of the ring so you know where to put your hook for Round 1.

Round 1 (RS): Ch4 (counts as 1dc and corner ch-sp), [3dc in ring, ch2] 3 times, 2dc in ring, slst in third ch of beginning ch4, slst in corner ch-sp. (12 dc and 4 corner ch-sps)

Round 2 (RS): Ch3 (counts as 1dc), [1dc, ch2, 2dc] in same corner sp, 1dc in each of next 3 sts, *[2dc, ch2, 2dc] in next corner sp, 1dc in each of next 3 sts; rep from * twice more, slst in third ch of beginning ch-3, slst in next dc, slst in corner ch-sp. (28 dc and 4 corner ch-sps)

Round 3 (RS): Ch3 (counts as 1dc), [1dc, ch2, 2dc] in same corner sp, 1dc in each dc to next corner, *[2dc, ch2, 2dc] in corner sp, 1dc in each dc to next corner; rep from * twice more, slst in third ch of beginning ch-3. (44 dc and 4 corner ch2-sps)

Fasten off with invisible fasten off, weave in ends.

JOINING

Join the squares as shown in the diagram above right.

EDGING

See Borders: Moss Stitch Border for a chart of this border.

On Round 1, count the joining seams and ch-sps of each motif as one stitch.

JOINING

Arrange the motifs as given in the diagram below. Using Bridal White, join the motifs with an invisible seam, such as mattress stitch, or you could join on the reverse with a single crochet seam (see Joining Techniques).

Round 1 (RS): Join Bridal White with slst to any corner ch-sp of cushion, ch1 (does not count as a st throughout), *[1sc, ch2, 1sc] in corner sp, ch1, skip 1 st, [1sc in next st, ch1, skip 1 st] to next corner sp of cushion; rep from * to end, slst in first sc, slst in corner ch-sp. (55 sts along each side, 4 corner ch2-sps)

Round 2 (RS): Ch1, *[1sc, ch2, 1sc] in corner sp, ch1, skip 1 st, [1sc in next ch1-sp, ch1, skip 1 st] to next corner sp; rep from * to end, slst in first sc, slst into corner ch-sp. (57 sts along each side, 4 corner ch2-sps)

Round 3 (RS): Rep Round 2. (59 sts along each side, 4 corner ch2-sps)

Fasten off.

Rep Rounds 1–3 in Icy Pink.

Rep Rounds 1–3 in Bridal White.

Rep Rounds 1–3 in Icy Blue.

Fasten off, weave in ends on wrong side.

FINISHING

Steam block your crochet cushion front, if needed.

Using matching sewing thread to cushion, hand stitch the crochet cushion front to the fabric cushion front, working small running stitches through the back of the crochet stitches.

USING COLOR

Choosing the right colors for your granny squares can feel overwhelming, because there are so many yarn and color choices. But mastering the art of using color can help transform your crochet projects from looking ordinary to looking extraordinary. The beauty of granny squares lies not only in their timeless pattern but also in the endless possibilities for color combinations. Whether you're creating a cozy blanket, a stylish bag, or a vibrant cushion, the colors you choose can make all the difference.

EMBRACE THE USE OF COLOR

- **A look at the process of color selection:** This will give you the knowledge and confidence to make your granny square projects truly stand out.
- **The basics of color theory:** An essential foundation that will help you understand how colors interact with each other.
- **Creating color palettes:** How to create palettes that are both beautiful and cohesive.
- **Showcase of some tried-and-tested color combinations:** Some combinations that work beautifully in granny squares, as well as inspiring examples of color use in classic, scrappy, and gradient designs.
- **Gaining confidence:** With this new-found knowledge, you'll soon feel confident in your color choices.

UNDERSTANDING COLOR THEORY

Before diving into color selection, it helps to understand the basics of color theory, and how the color wheel can help us with our color choices.

THE COLOR WHEEL

This is a visual representation of colors arranged in a circle, showing the relationships between primary colors (red, blue, yellow), secondary colors (green, orange, purple), and tertiary colors (mixes of primary and secondary colors, such as yellow-green, blue-violet, red-orange).

COLOR TEMPERATURE

Warm colors (reds, oranges, yellows) remind us of fire and heat, and are vivid and energetic. Using these colors in our crochet can help make a project feel cozy and inviting. On the other hand, cool colors (blues, greens, purples) give an impression of calm and create a soothing vibe. Using these in our crochet can help make a project feel serene.

COLOR VALUES

This refers to the lightness or darkness of a color. A color can have lots of values, which creates an even wider choice for our crochet, because yarn also comes in lots of different shades, tones, and tints.

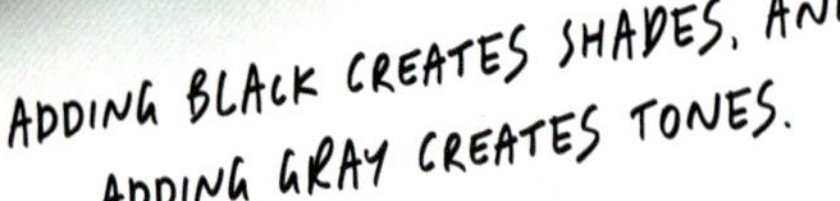

COLOR RELATIONSHIPS

You can mix these relationships up a little, too, to create your own palette, such as three analogous colors with a complementary color (so maybe blue, blue-violet, and violet with yellow-orange).

- **Complementary colors:** Colors that are opposite each other on the color wheel create a vibrant and vivid look (for example, red and green or orange and blue).
- **Analogous colors:** Colors that sit next to each other on the color wheel create a harmonious blend (such as orange, yellow, and green).
- **Triadic colors:** Three colors evenly spaced around the wheel offer a balanced and dynamic palette (for example, red, yellow, and blue).
- **Tetradic colors:** Four colors evenly spaced around the wheel also offer a balanced and dynamic palette (for example, red, yellow, green, and purple).

CREATING HARMONIOUS COLOR PALETTES

Choosing colors that work well together is an art, but these tips can help.

HOW TO GET STARTED

- **Select a dominant color for your project:** This could be your favorite color or one that matches your décor.
- **Add complementary colors:** Choose one or two colors that complement your main color. Use the color wheel to find these.
- **Include neutrals:** Adding white, black, gray, or beige can balance brighter colors and prevent your project from becoming too overwhelming.
- **Experiment with color value:** Use different shades and tints of your chosen colors to add depth and interest to your project.
- **Consider the mood:** Think about the mood you want to convey. Warm colors can make your project feel lively and energetic, while cool colors can create a peaceful and relaxing effect.

PRACTICAL TIPS FOR COLOR SELECTION

- **Use a color wheel:** Keep a color wheel handy to help you visualize and select harmonious colors.
- **Look for inspiration:** Nature, artwork, fabric, and home décor can provide excellent color combinations. Don't be afraid to take photos of things you find inspiring when you're out and about.
- **Test with swatches:** Crochet small swatches or use a design app to test different color combinations before starting your project.
- **Limit your palette:** Too many colors can make a design look chaotic. Stick to 3–5 colors for a balanced look.
- **Think about placement:** The placement of colors in your granny squares can affect the overall look. Experiment with different arrangements to see what looks best.
- **Consider the yarn texture:** Different yarn textures can affect how colors appear. A shiny yarn might make colors look more vibrant, while a matte yarn can give a more subdued effect.

USING COLOR PEGS

A great way to play around with color is to create small yarn pegs, by wrapping oddments of colorful yarn around wooden pegs. I find yarn pegs such a valuable tool in helping me choose the right combination of colors for my projects, and they're a great way to use up oddments of yarn, as well as being great fun to play around with. Take photos of your favorite combinations so that you don't forget them.

COLOR COMBINATIONS FOR GRANNY SQUARES

Using color effectively in your granny squares can elevate your crochet projects to new heights as well as bringing you joy throughout the making process. To help you on your creative journey, here are some tried-and-true color combinations to get you started.

CLASSIC COMBINATIONS

- Red, Navy, and White
- Shades of Pink and White
- Mint, Peach, and Gold

MODERN COMBINATIONS

- Gray, Mustard, and White
- Teal, Coral, and Navy
- Mint, Peach, and Gold

NATURE-INSPIRED

- **Earth tones:** Brown, Green, and Tan
- **Ocean tones:** Blue, Aqua, and Sand
- **Floral tones:** Pink, Yellow, and Green

SEASONAL THEMES

- **Spring:** Pastel shades of Pink, Green, and Yellow
- **Summer:** Bright shades of Orange, Pink, and Turquoise
- **Autumn:** Warm shades of Orange, Brown, and Red
- **Winter:** Cool shades of Blue, Silver, and White

EXAMPLES OF COLOR USE IN CLASSIC GRANNY SQUARES

CLASSIC GRANNY SQUARE

Use a single color for the center, another for the middle rounds, and a third for the outer edge. This gives a structured and symmetrical look.

SCRAPPY GRANNY SQUARE

Use leftover yarns of various colors. This is a great way to create a vibrant and eclectic design.

GRADIENT GRANNY SQUARE

Use different shades of a single color, from light to dark, to create a gradient effect. This adds a sophisticated and cohesive look to your project.

JOINING TECHNIQUES

Once you have mastered the art of granny square crochet, the next step is to join your motifs to create larger projects. Joining seamlessly and professionally will help to showcase your skills, as well as helping you create pieces that will stand the test of time (and regular washing). This can seem a daunting task, especially when you are new to crochet, but the great thing about crochet is that there are lots of ways to do the same thing, which means that you can find the method that suits you best.

FIND THE BEST JOIN

- **Different methods:** I have covered four different ways of joining. Each offers its own unique benefits and visual appeal, allowing you to choose the method that best suits your project's design and construction needs.
- **Seamless finish:** Try a sewn whip stitch.
- **For simplicity:** A crocheted join is the best choice.
- **Set yourself a challenge:** Have a go at join-as-you-go.
- **Instructions:** You'll find all the instructions in this chapter to guide you through each process, so that you can turn your granny motifs into handmade treasures.

SIMPLE JOINING TECHNIQUES

Whichever method you choose, when joining motifs you will need to sew seams in different orientations (vertically, horizontally—and diagonally for some motifs). First you will need to join all the seams in one direction, then join the seams in the other direction.

WHIP STITCH / OVERSEWING

Place the motif edges to be joined side by side, with the the right side uppermost, and use a matching yarn for an almost invisible seam, or a contrasting color yarn for a decorative seam.

Step 1: Thread a yarn needle with a long length of yarn and, starting at one end of the seam, thread the needle through the inner loops of the stitch only (the loops that are adjacent) **(A)**. Pull the yarn through, leaving a short tail to weave in later.

Step 2: Insert the needle through the inner loops only of the next stitch on each edge and pull the yarn through.

Step 3: Repeat Step 2 until the seam is joined **(B)**.

Step 4: Pick up the next two motifs and join in the same way. Continue until all required motifs and seams are joined.

A

B

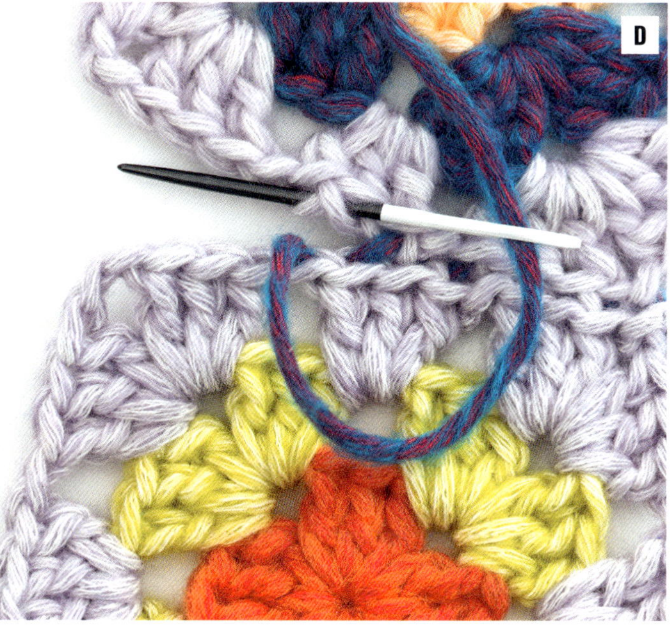

MATTRESS STITCH / LADDER STITCH

Place the motif edges to be joined side by side, with the the right side uppermost, and use a matching yarn or a similar shade of yarn. This is an invisible seam, so the color you use is not critical.

Step 1: Thread a yarn needle with a long length of yarn and, starting at one end of the seam, thread the needle down through the center of the first stitch on one motif and up through center of the next stitch on the same motif, then pull the yarn through.

Step 2: Take the needle to the opposite motif, thread the needle down through the center of the first stitch on the opposite motif and up through center of next stitch on same motif **(C)**, then pull yarn through.

Step 3: Repeat Step 2 until the seam is joined **(D)**.

Step 4: Pick up the next two motifs and join in the same way. Continue until all required motifs and seams are joined.

SINGLE CROCHET SEAM

Place the motif edges to be joined side by side, with the the right side uppermost, and use a matching yarn for a blended seam, or a contrasting color yarn for a decorative seam.

Step 1: With a slip knot on your hook, insert your crochet hook through the left-most corner stitch of both squares **(A)**. Yarn over, pull through both loops (you will have two loops on your hook). Yarn over again and pull through both loops to complete the single crochet stitch **(B)**.

Step 2: Continue working single crochet to join the squares, working into the inner (adjacent) loops only of the corresponding stitches **(C)**, ending with a single crochet in the opposite corner space.

Step 3: When the seam is joined, ch1, pick up the next two motifs and join in the same way, with a single crochet in each corner sp and in the inner loops only of stitches.

Continue until all required motifs are joined.

D

SLIP STITCH SEAM

Can be worked on the right side or the wrong side of the work. Place the motif edges to be joined side by side. Wrong sides together will create a join on the right side of work, and right sides together will create a join on the wrong side of the work. Use a matching yarn for a blended seam, or a contrasting color yarn for a decorative seam.

Step 1: With a slip knot on your hook, insert your crochet hook through the left-most corner stitch of both squares **(D)**. Yarn over, and pull through all loops. You will have one loop on your hook and the slip stitch is complete **(E)**.

Step 2: Continue working slip stitch to join the squares, working into the inner (adjacent) loops only of the corresponding stitches **(F)**, ending with a slip stitch in the opposite corner sp.

Step 3: When the seam is joined, ch1, pick up the next two motifs and join in the same way, with a slip stitch in each corner sp and in the inner loops only of the stitches.

Continue until all the required motifs are joined.

NOTE: *For a more sturdy join, or to make the join stand out as a feature, you can insert hook under both loops of the stitch with this seam.*

E

F

JOIN-AS-YOU-GO

This method is a great way to join with a flat, almost invisible seam. It involves the technique of joining your motifs as you are crocheting the final round, and it may seem tricky at first. But once you master this technique you'll love it, because it doesn't interrupt the overall visual appearance of a larger project.

CLASSIC GRANNY MOTIF JOIN-AS-YOU-GO

Whilst the specific details should be included within the pattern, here is a guide to the join-as-you-go technique for a classic granny square, which you can refer to whenever you need it.

Step 1: Complete your first motif to the end, as per the pattern, including the final round.

Step 2: Work your next motif until the final round. This motif is now the working motif.

Step 3: Complete the first side of your final round, until you reach the next corner. Do not work the corner **(A)**.

Step 4: Work the first half of the corner only. For example if your corner consists of [3dc, ch2, 3dc] you would work half of this, which is 3dc and ch1 **(B)**.

Step 5: Insert the hook from bottom to top, through the corresponding corner of the motif being joined (this is called the joining motif), yarn over **(C)**, and pull back through the corner and the loop on the hook to make a slst. The slst replaces the next corner ch1. The two squares are now joined at the corner.

Step 6: Work your next group of 3dc on the working motif to complete the corner **(D)**.

Step 7: Replace the next ch1 with a slst in the corresponding space on the opposite (joining) motif **(E)**.

Step 8: Work your next group of 3dc in the next ch1-sp along the side of the working motif.

Continue working in this way, repeating Steps 7 and 8 **(F)**, until you have completed the final slst along the side. Repeat Steps 4-6 to join the next corner. The two motifs are now joined along one side.

Complete the final round of the working motif.

To make a strip of squares you repeat this process, joining one side of the motifs in the same way on the final round.

When you start to build up rows of joined motifs, you will need to join two or more sides on some motifs, which simply means you will join extra sides and extra corners as required.

To join four corners, join the working motif to the joining motif as before, until two corners are joined. Work a slst into the corner of the motif directly above the working motif. Complete the final round of the working motif.

DOUBLE CROCHET JOIN-AS-YOU-GO

The join-as-you-go method is slightly different when the final round of a motif is a single stitch, such as a double crochet in every stitch or space along the sides.

Step 1: Follow the steps for Classic Granny Motif Join-as-you-go up to the end of Step 4 **(A)**.

Step 2: Insert the hook from top to bottom through the corresponding corner of the motif being joined **(B)** (this is called the joining motif), make a slst, then ch1 **(C)**. The two squares are now joined at the corner.

Step 3: Work 2dc in the corner of the working motif to complete the corner as follows: *1dc, remove the hook from working loop, insert hook from top to bottom through the corresponding dc of the motif being joined **(D)**, replace the working loop on the hook and pull through the stitch **(E)***; rep from * to * once more in the corner space, then rep from * to * in every dc to the next corner ch-sp **(F)**.

Step 4: Repeat Step 2, then repeat Step 3 until the corner stitches are complete. The two motifs are now joined along one side.

Complete the final round of the working motif.

To make a strip of squares you repeat this process, joining one side of motifs in the same way on the final round.

When you start to build up rows of joined motifs, you will need to join two or more sides on some motifs, which simply means you will join extra sides and extra corners as required.

To join four corners, join the working motif to the joining motif as before, until two corners are joined. Work a slst into the corner of the motif directly above the working motif. Complete the final round of the working motif.

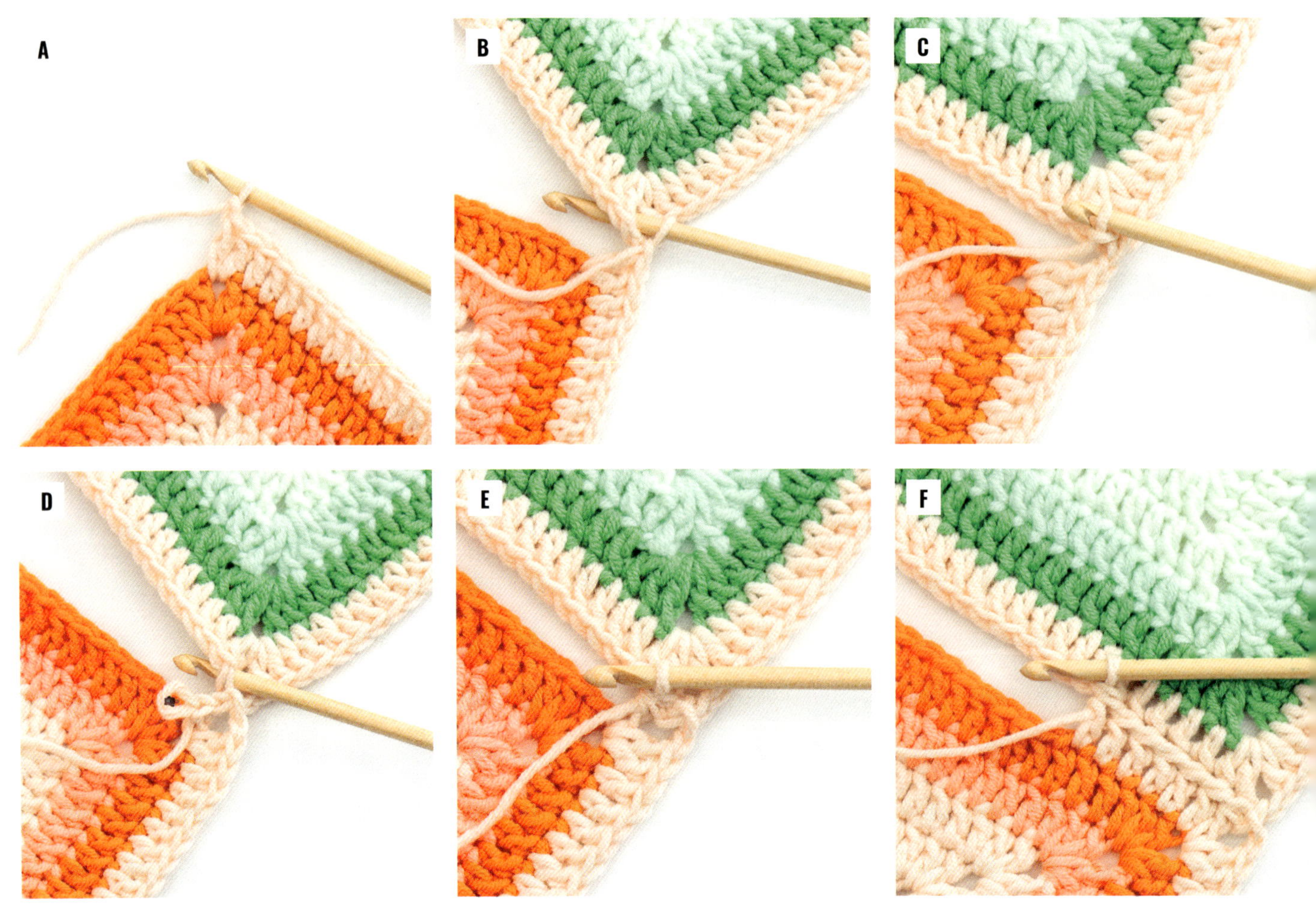

BORDERS

Sometimes less is more, and when you've crocheted a beautiful and colorful granny square project, such as a blanket, the best way to finish it off is to add a simple border edge that complements both the colors and stitch patterns used. Alternatively, if the project itself is very simple, you may feel that a decorative border will add some extra detail or provide a focal point or striking feature.

FINISHING THE EDGE

- **Crochet borders:** These can help to neaten up the edges of a project, creating a professional looking finish.
- **Choosing the right border:** I have included a selection of edgings that range from simple to more advanced, so that you can build up your skills and techniques, and experiment with different stitches and border styles.

DOUBLE CROCHET BORDER

Using a single stitch to create a border around a square is one of the simplest ways to add a neat edging. You can work one round, or more, depending on how deep you would like your border to be. This example uses double crochet, but you can replace this with any stitch—such as half double crochet, or single crochet.

YOU WILL NEED

Yarn

Use the same weight of yarn as for your project

Hook

Hook size recommended for your yarn

PATTERN

Join yarn with slst to any corner ch-sp of project.

Round 1 (RS): Ch3 (counts as first dc), [1dc, ch2, 2dc] in same corner, 1dc in every st or sp along first side, *[2dc, ch2, 2dc] in next corner, 1dc in every st or sp along next side; rep from * to end, slst in top of third ch of beginning ch-3.

Fasten off.

Rep Round 1 as many times as desired, using a different color for each round.

TOP TIP

If your edges become wavy, you have too many stitches, or your stitches are too loose. Try working fewer stitches in the corners for a few rounds (for example [2dc, ch2, 2dc]), or go down a hook size.

To create a different texture for added interest, try working your border stitches into the back loops only (see Bright Squares Baby Blanket).

CHART

STRETCHY RIBBED EDGE

When you crochet garments, it's great to add a neat and stretchy ribbed edging. You add this edging to the edge stitches of a project, and work in rows to create a classic-looking rib. In this example we use ch15, but this may vary depending on how deep you would like your rib to be.

YOU WILL NEED

Yarn

Use the same weight of yarn as for your project

Hook

Hook size recommended for your yarn

PATTERN

Join yarn with slst to any st along edge of project.

Row 1 (RS): Ch15, 1sc in second ch from hook, 1sc in each ch to end, slst in each of next 2 sts along main edge, turn. (14 sts)

Row 2 (WS): Skip last 2 slsts, 1scBLO in each st to last st, 1sc in last st, turn.

Row 3 (RS): Ch1 (does not count as a st), 1sc in first st, 1scBLO in each st to end, slst in next 2 sts on main edge, turn.

Rep Rows 2 and 3 around until all sts of edge are used up.

Fasten off.

CHART

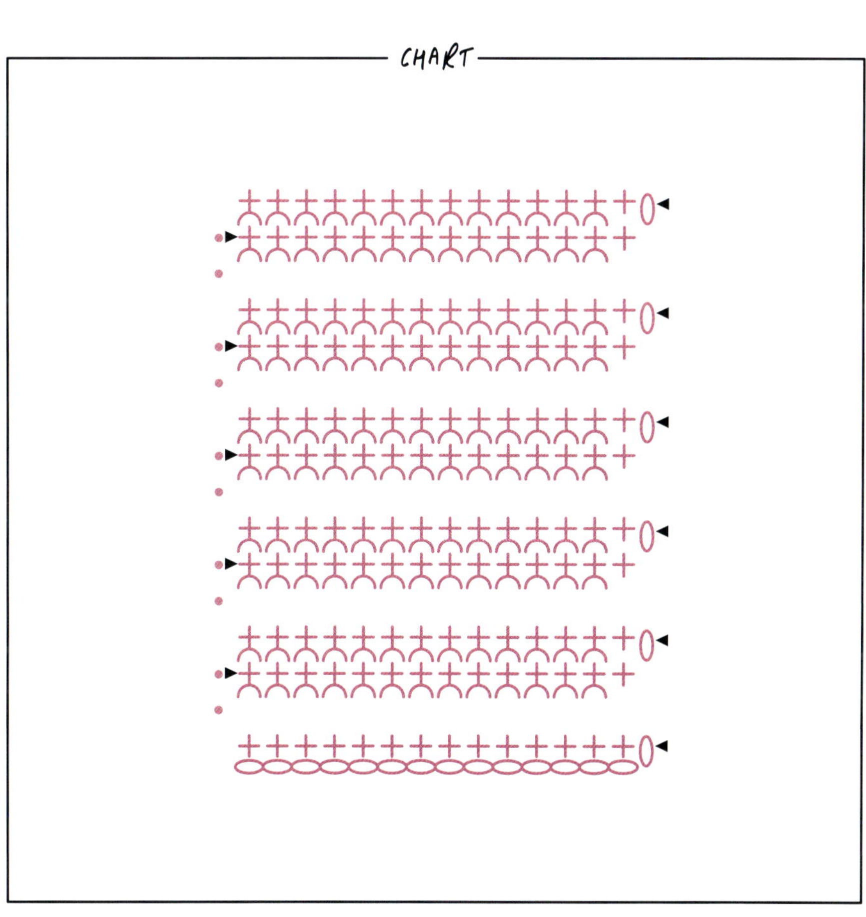

SHELL STITCH BORDER

One of my favorite edgings to finish off a cozy blanket is this pretty scalloped edging, which uses basic crochet stitches including double crochet, half double crochet, single crochet, slip stitch, and chains.

YOU WILL NEED

Yarn

Use the same weight of yarn as for your project in two different colors, Color 1 and Color 2—or use colors as instructed in the pattern

Hook

Hook size recommended for your yarn

PATTERN

Join Color 1 with slst to any corner sp.

Round 1 (RS): Ch3 (counts as first dc), 4dc in same corner sp, 1dc in every st and sp to next corner sp, *5dc in corner sp, 1dc in every st and sp to next corner sp; rep from * twice more, slst in third ch of beginning ch-3 to join.

Fasten off.

Round 2 (RS): Join Color 2 with slst to first dc of any corner, *ch5, skip next 3 dc, slst in next dc; rep from * to last 3 dc, ch5, skip next 3 dc, slst in base of beginning ch-5.

Cut yarn and fasten off.

Round 3 (RS): Join Color 1 with slst to any ch5-sp, ch1 (does not count as a st) *[1sc, 1hdc, 1dc, ch2, 1dc, 1hdc, 1sc] all in ch5-sp (working over ch-5 loop and not in any individual sts); rep from * in every ch5-sp to end, slst in first sc.

Fasten off.

TOP TIP

Don't worry if you reach the end of one side and you don't quite have the right number of stitches to skip, as it won't be noticeable in your finished border if you skip one stitch less here and there.

CHART

MOSS STITCH BORDER

This is one of my favorite stitches, so I love to use it as a border, too. It provides a beautiful woven texture and is really easy to crochet. Note that this stitch can sometimes feel tight, so you will need to check your work as you crochet and go up a hook size if needed.

YOU WILL NEED

Yarn

Use the same weight of yarn as for your project, in several colors

Hook

Hook size recommended for your yarn

PATTERN

Join yarn with slst to any corner ch-sp of project. You will first create a foundation round.

Foundation round: Ch1 (does not count as a st throughout), [2sc, ch2, 2sc] in same corner, 1sc in every st or sp along first side, *[2sc, ch2, 2sc] in next corner, 1sc in every st or sp along next side; rep from * to end, slst in top of first sc, slst in corner sp.

Round 1 (RS): Ch1, *[1sc, ch2, 1sc] in corner sp, ch1, skip 1 st, [1sc in next st, ch1, skip 1 st] to next corner sp; rep from * to end, slst in first sc, slst in corner ch-sp.

Round 2 (RS): Ch1, *[1sc, ch2, 1sc] in corner sp, ch1, skip 1 st, [1sc in next ch1-sp, ch1, skip 1 st] to next corner sp; rep from * to end, slst in first sc, slst in corner ch-sp.

Rep Round 2 until you reach your desired depth of border.

You can change your color as you please. You will produce a different effect with 1, 2 or 3 rounds of each color, so have a play around with it and see what you think!

Fasten off.

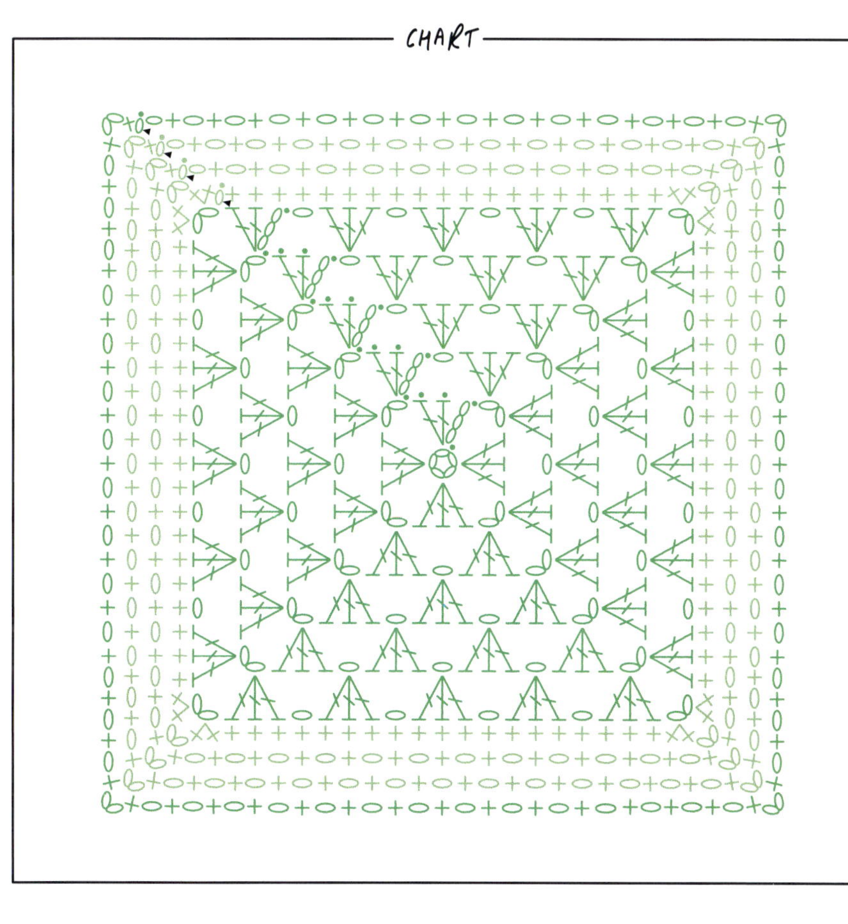

TECHNIQUES

Whether you're picking up a hook for the first time or need a refresher, this chapter will equip you with the skills to tackle the motifs and patterns in this book with confidence. I've covered all the essential stitches and techniques you'll need to create your beautiful crochet projects.

BASIC STITCHES TO INTRICATE TECHNIQUES

- **Step-by-step instructions:** These will give you a solid foundation that you can build on, as your crochet goes from strength to strength.
- **Illustrations:** Each step has an accompanying illustration so you can see exactly what to do.
- **Abbreviations:** This section also explains all the abbreviations used in this book.
- **Reference:** Use this section as a handy guide whenever you are not sure of a particular stitch.

ABBREVIATIONS

3tr-CL	3 treble cluster
BLO	back loop only
bb	back bump
ch	chain
ch-sp(s)	chain space(s)
CL	cluster
dc	double crochet
dc2tog	work 2 double crochet sts together (decrease 1 st)
FLO	front loop only
hdc	half double crochet
rep	repeat
RS	right side
sc	single crochet
sc2tog	work 2 single crochet sts together (decrease 1 st)
slst	slip stitch
st(s)	stitch(es)
tr	treble crochet
WS	wrong side
yoh	yarn over hook

US/UK CONVERSIONS

US	**UK**
Single crochet (sc)	Double crochet (dc)
Half double crochet (hdc)	Half treble crochet (htr)
Double crochet (dc)	Treble crochet (tr)
Treble crochet (tr)	Double treble crochet (dtr)
Yarn over hook (yoh)	Yarn round hook (yrh)

SLIP KNOT

Step 1: Make a loop with the yarn, crossing the working yarn over the tail end **(A)**.

Step 2: Pull through a loop of yarn from the working yarn, to make a slip knot **(B)**.

Step 3: Place the slip knot on your hook and then tighten it and move it up towards the tip of your hook, by pulling the yarn ends.

Step 4: The knot is now sitting against your hook and your slip knot is complete **(C)**.

CHAIN STITCH (CH OR CHS)

Step 1: Begin with a slip knot on your hook. Bring your working yarn over your index finger and hold the tail end of the yarn with your middle finger and thumb, immediately underneath the slip knot. Take the yarn over the hook **(D)**.

Step 2: Holding the tail end of yarn tightly, pull the hook and yarn towards you and through the loop on the hook **(E)**.

Step 3: There is now a stitch sitting below the hook, above the slip knot. This is your first chain **(F)**.

Step 4: Repeat for as many chains as you require. After working a few chain stitches, move your finger and thumb up to grasp the chain directly beneath the hook. This helps you to control your crochet more easily.

Step 5: The chain stitches will look like interlocking Vs and each of these V-shaped stitches is 1 chain stitch **(G)**.

NUMBER OF TURNING CHAINS

US	UK	CHAINS
Single crochet (sc)	Double crochet (dc)	1 chain
Half double crochet (hdc)	Half treble crochet (htr)	2 chains
Double crochet (dc)	Treble crochet (tr)	3 chains

TURNING CHAINS (OR BEGINNING CHAINS)

The turning or beginning chain at the start of a row or round generally matches the height of the stitches that follow it, so it will usually consist of the number of chains shown in the table above.

The pattern will tell you how many chains to begin with, and whether they count as a stitch or not.

SLIP STITCH (SLST)

Step 1: Insert the hook into the stitch or space indicated. Take the yarn over the hook **(H)**.

Step 2: Pull the yarn back through the stitch or space, and also through the loop on the hook, to complete the slip stitch **(I)**.

JOINING A NEW COLOR WITH A SLIP STITCH

Step 1: Make a slip knot on the hook with the new yarn. Insert the hook from front to back through the stitch or space indicated **(J)**.

Step 2: Take the yarn over the hook and pull it back through the stitch or space and also through the loop on the hook, to complete the slip stitch and join the new color **(K)**.

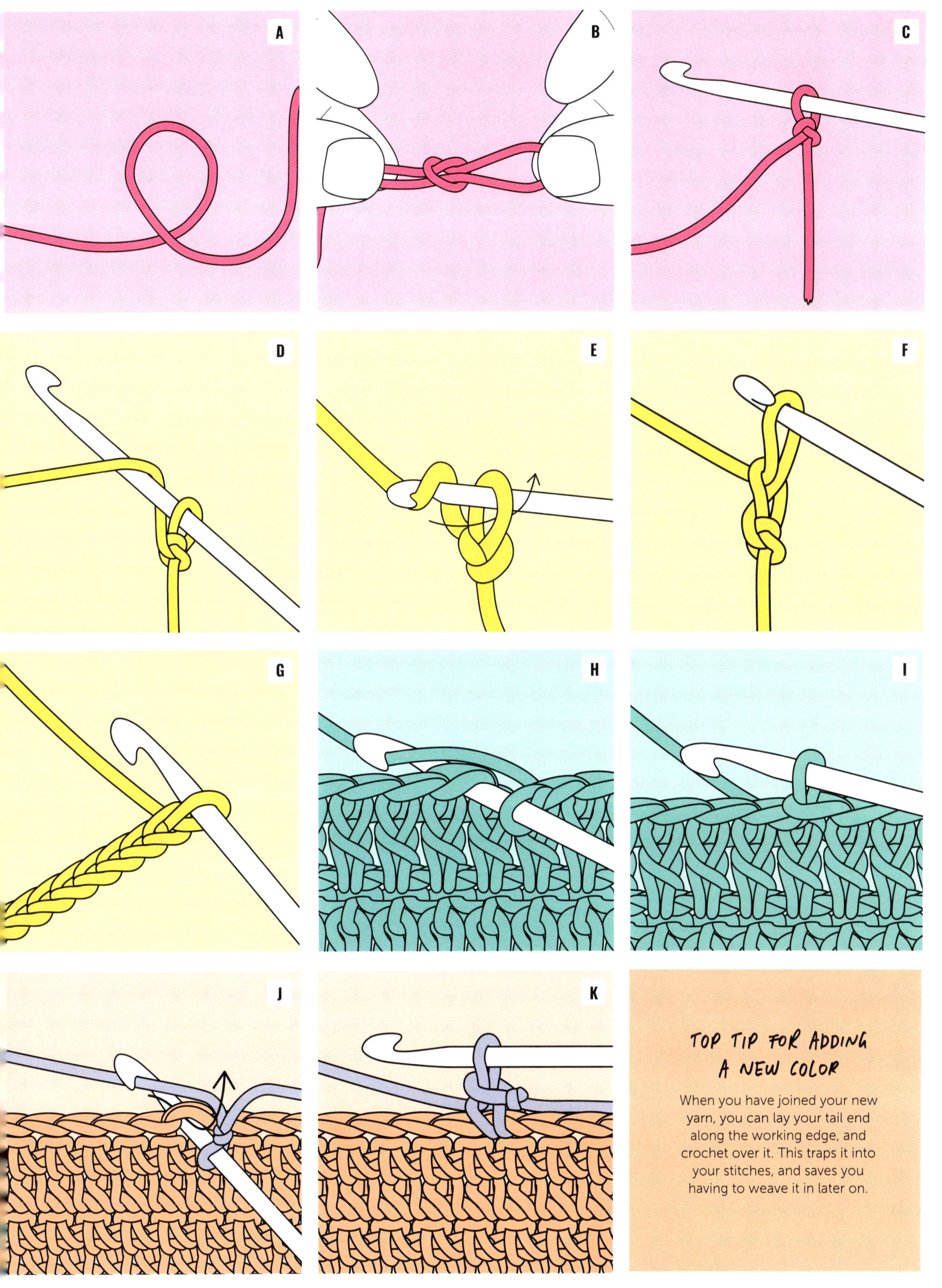

TOP TIP FOR ADDING A NEW COLOR

When you have joined your new yarn, you can lay your tail end along the working edge, and crochet over it. This traps it into your stitches, and saves you having to weave it in later on.

CHAIN RING

Step 1: Make a slip knot on your hook.

Step 2: Make the number of chains as indicated in your pattern instructions **(A)**. 5 chains is good for a beginner, and 4 chains can also be used.

Step 3: Insert your hook in the first of these chains and make a slip stitch to form a ring **(B)**. For the first round you will place your hook in the center of the ring **(C)**.

MAGIC RING

Step 1: Follow Steps 1 and 2 for making a slip knot. Do not pull the slip knot tight **(D)**. Place the large loop of yarn on your hook, with a twist to the left of the hook. This is your magic ring (or adjustable ring).

Step 2: Insert the hook into the loop of the loose slip knot and hold the loose center with your middle finger and thumb as you put your working yarn into position over the second finger **(E)**.

Step 3: Work over the twisted yarn of the slip knot as you work your first round into the center of the ring **(F)**.

Step 4: Pull the tail end tight to close the ring **(G)**.

SINGLE CROCHET (SC)

Step 1: Insert the hook into the stitch or space indicated. Take yarn over the hook **(H)**.

Step 2: Pull the yarn back through the stitch or space (2 loops are on your hook). Yarn over hook again **(I)**.

Step 3: Pull the yarn through both loops on the hook to complete the single crochet stitch **(J)**.

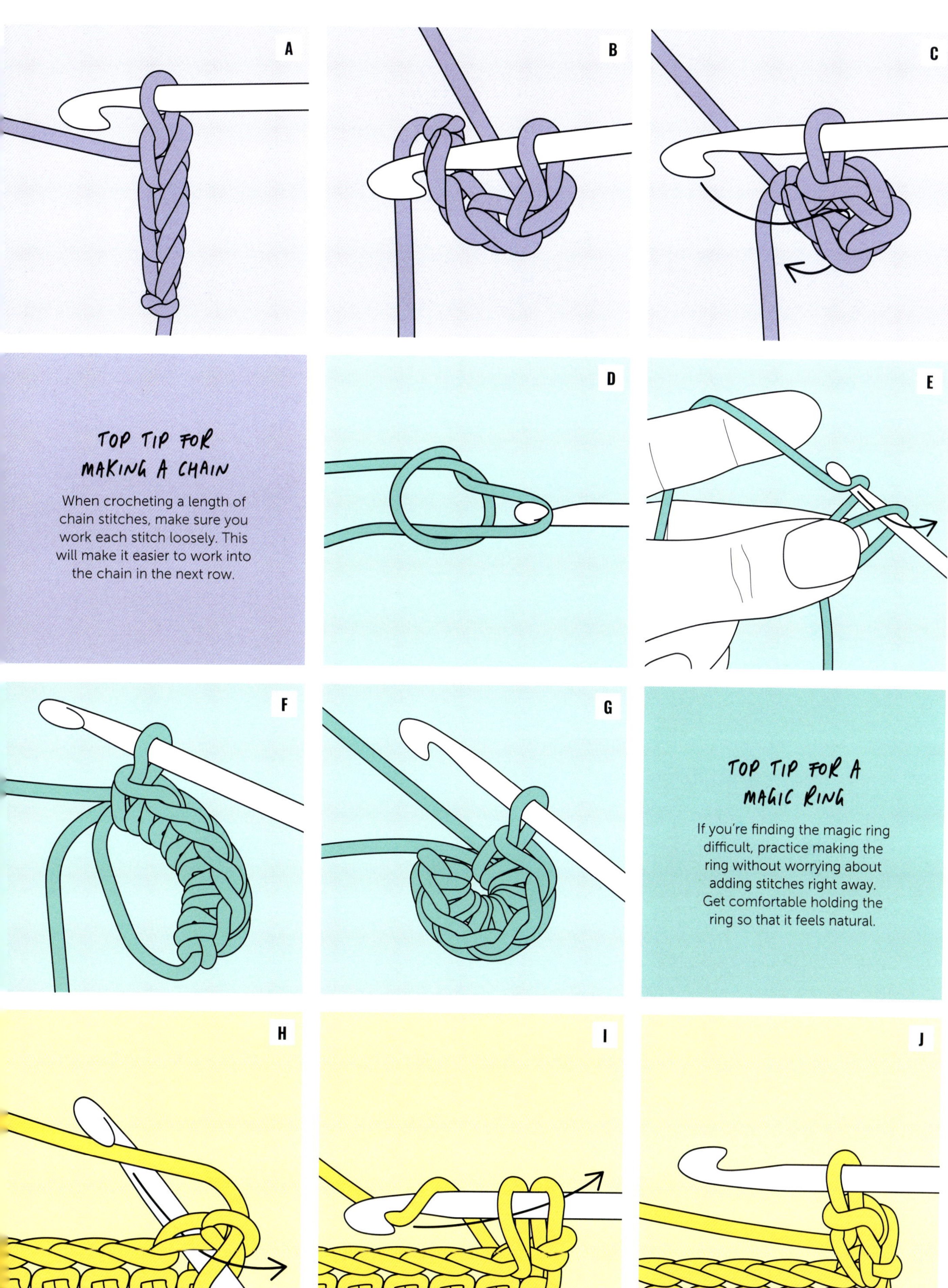

TOP TIP FOR MAKING A CHAIN

When crocheting a length of chain stitches, make sure you work each stitch loosely. This will make it easier to work into the chain in the next row.

TOP TIP FOR A MAGIC RING

If you're finding the magic ring difficult, practice making the ring without worrying about adding stitches right away. Get comfortable holding the ring so that it feels natural.

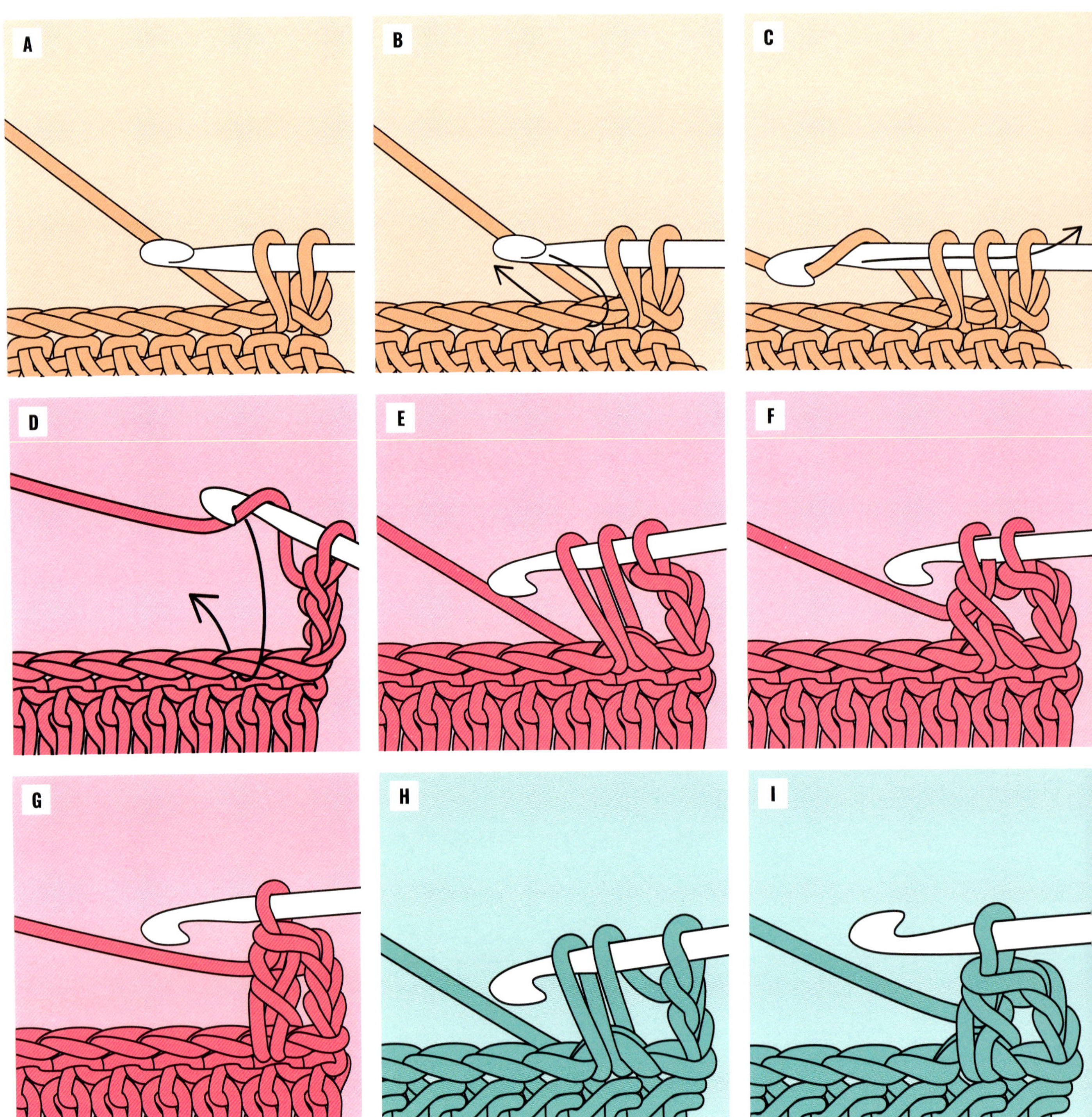
A
B
C
D
E
F
G
H
I

SINGLE CROCHET DECREASE (SINGLE CROCHET 2 STITCHES TOGETHER SC2TOG)

Step 1: Insert the hook into the stitch or space indicated. Take the yarn over the hook and pull the yarn back through the stitch or space (2 loops are on your hook) **(A)**.

Step 2: Insert your hook into the next stitch or space indicated **(B)**.

Step 3: Yarn over hook and pull the yarn back through the stitch or space (3 loops are on your hook) **(C)**. Take the yarn over the hook again and pull the yarn through all 3 loops to complete the stitch.

DOUBLE CROCHET (DC)

Step 1: Take the yarn over the hook. Insert the hook into the stitch or space indicated **(D)**.

Step 2: Yarn over hook again and pull the yarn back through the stitch or space (3 loops are on your hook) **(E)**.

Step 3: Take the yarn over the hook again and pull it through the first 2 loops on the hook (2 loops remain on your hook) **(F)**.

Step 4: Yarn over hook again and pull it through the last 2 loops on the hook to complete the double crochet stitch **(G)**.

HALF DOUBLE CROCHET (HDC)

Step 1: Follow Steps 1 and 2 for double crochet (3 loops are on your hook) **(H)**.

Step 2: Take the yarn over the hook again and pull it through all 3 loops to complete the half double crochet stitch **(I)**.

TREBLE CROCHET (TR)

Step 1: Take the yarn over the hook twice. Insert the hook into the stitch or space indicated **(A)**.

Step 2: Yarn over hook again and pull the yarn back through the stitch or space (4 loops are on your hook) **(B)**.

Step 3: Take the yarn over the hook again and pull it through the first 2 loops on the hook as shown **(C)**.

Step 4: You'll now have 3 loops on the hook. Yarn over hook again and pull it through the first 2 loops on the hook **(D)**.

Step 5: Two loops remain on your hook. Yarn over hook and pull it through the last 2 loops on the hook **(E)** to complete the treble crochet stitch.

THREE TREBLE CROCHET CLUSTER STITCH (3TR-CL)

Step 1: Take the yarn over the hook twice. Insert the hook into the stitch or space indicated **(F)**.

Step 2: Yarn over the hook again and pull a loop back through the stitch or space (4 loops are on the hook) **(G)**.

Step 3: [Yarn over hook again and pull through 2 loops] twice (2 loops remain on the hook) **(H)**.

Step 4: Repeat Steps 1–3, twice more, working into the same stitch or space each time (4 loops are now on the hook) **(I)**.

Step 5: Yarn over hook and pull through 4 loops to complete the 3tr-cl **(J)**.

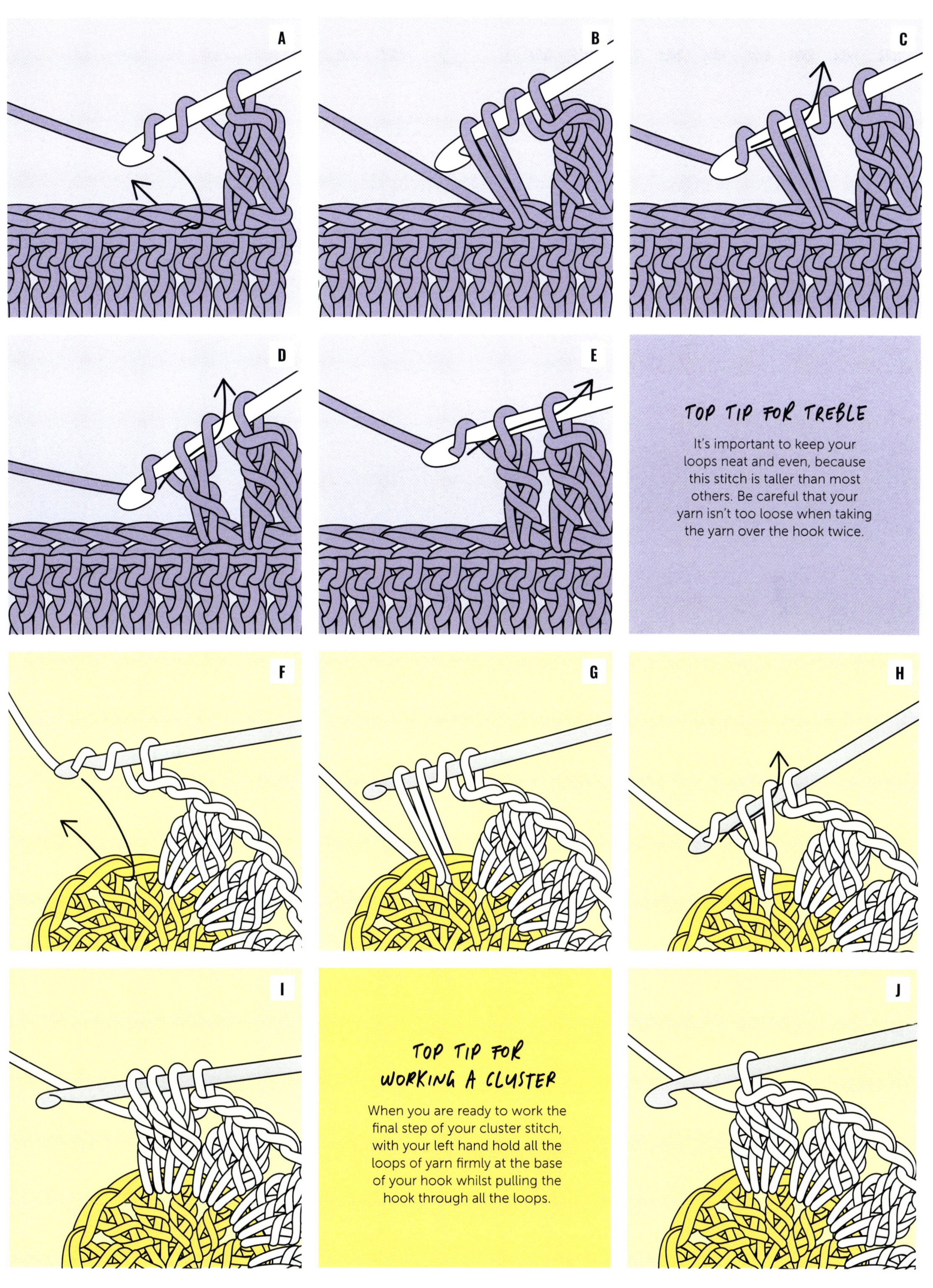

TOP TIP FOR TREBLE

It's important to keep your loops neat and even, because this stitch is taller than most others. Be careful that your yarn isn't too loose when taking the yarn over the hook twice.

TOP TIP FOR WORKING A CLUSTER

When you are ready to work the final step of your cluster stitch, with your left hand hold all the loops of yarn firmly at the base of your hook whilst pulling the hook through all the loops.

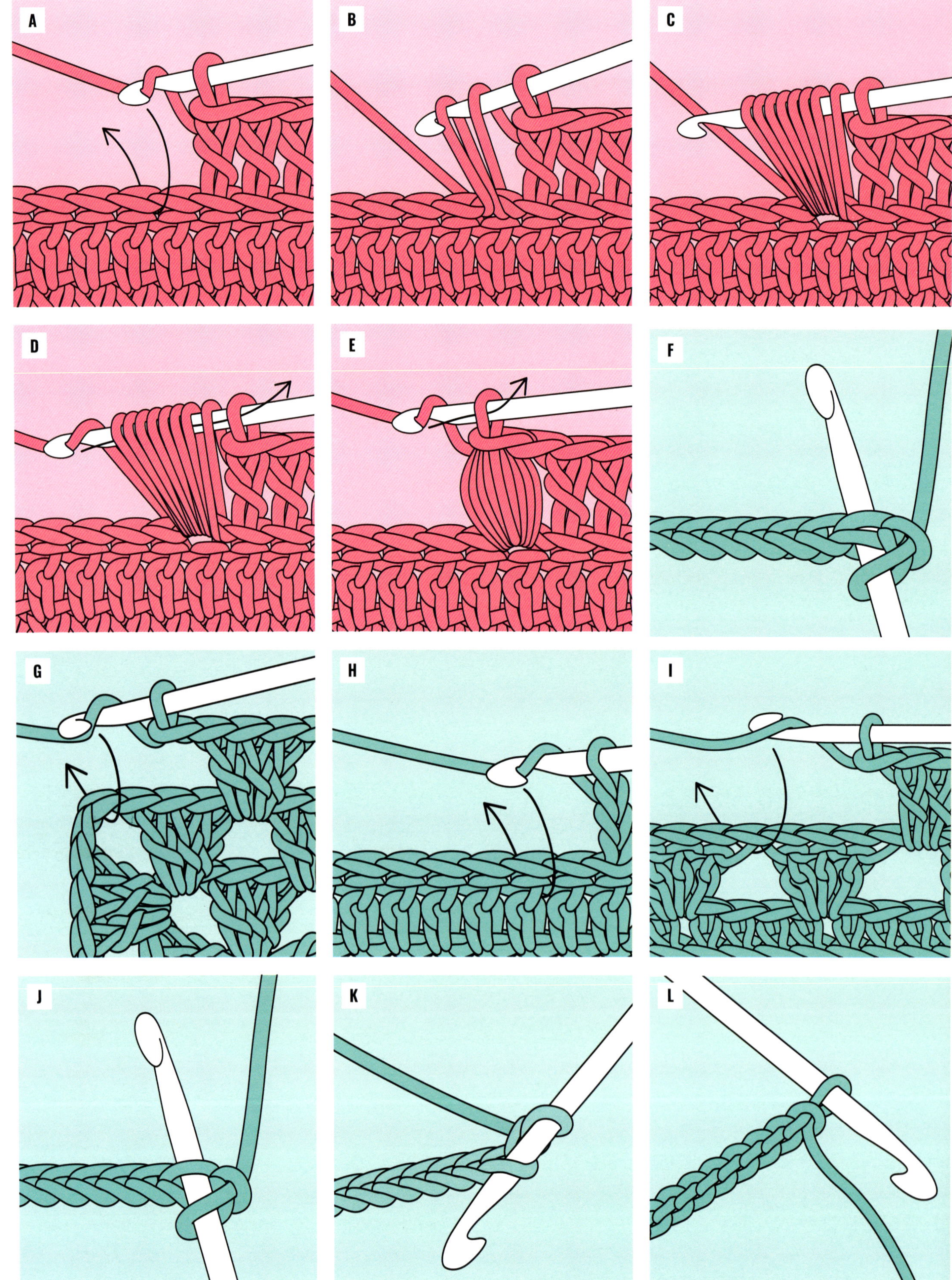
A
B
C
D
E
F
G
H
I
J
K
L

PUFF STITCH (PUFF-ST)

Step 1: Take the yarn over the hook, then insert the hook into the stitch or space indicated **(A)**.

Step 2: Yarn over hook again and pull a loop back through the stitch or space (3 loops are on the hook) **(B)**.

Step 3: Making sure you keep your loops loose, repeat Steps 1 and 2 a further 3 times into the same stitch or space (9 loops are on the hook) **(C)**.

Step 4: Take the yarn over the hook and carefully pull through all 9 loops on the hook **(D)**.

Step 5: Ch1 to close the puff stitch **(E)**. Note that this ch1 is part of the puff stitch and not part of any instructions that may follow.

PLACING YOUR STITCHES

Regular crochet

Unless indicated otherwise, always place your hook under two loops of a stitch **(F)**.

Working into a chain space

Insert your hook into the space that sits below the chain stitch or stitches **(G)**.

Working in between stitches

Insert your hook into the space between two stitches (and not into the top of a stitch) **(H)**.

Working in between groups of stitches

Insert your hook in the gap or chain space between groups of stitches (as with the granny stitch) **(I)**.

Working in Back Loop Only (BLO)

Instead of inserting the hook under both top loops of a stitch, insert the hook under the back loop of the stitch only **(J)**.

Working in Front Loop Only (FLO)

Instead of inserting the hook under both top loops of a stitch, insert the hook under the front loop of the stitch only **(K)**.

Working into back bump of a stitch (bb)

This back bump is situated behind the top of the stitch. It is a small horizontal loop that sits at the back **(L)**.

JOINING THE ROUND

Step 1: When you have completed your final stitch of the round, insert your hook into the top chain of your beginning chain, or into the first stitch of the round. Your pattern will tell you where to join. Make sure you insert your hook under two loops of the chain stitch, or under the two loops of the stitch. This will avoid an unsightly large loop forming **(A)**.

Step 2: Yarn over hook and pull the loop back though the stitch and through the loop on the hook to complete the slip stitch **(B)**.

INVISIBLE FASTEN OFF

Step 1: Join the round as indicated in the pattern. Remove the hook from the working loop and turn your motif over so that wrong side is facing. Insert the hook into the top of the next stitch (under both loops of the stitch), to the right of the working loop **(C)**.

Step 2: Replace the working loop back on the hook **(D)**.

Step 3: Pull the yarn tight, then pull the working loop through the top of the stitch. Cut the yarn leaving a tail of approximately 5–6in (12–15cm). Yarn over hook and pull the yarn tail all the way through the loop on the hook **(E)**. Tighten up the knot and turn the motif to the right side.

WEAVING IN ENDS

When fastening off, try to leave at least 5–6in (12–15cm) of yarn where possible, on the wrong side of the work.

Step 1: Thread the yarn tail onto a yarn needle. Thread the needle through the base of the closest stitches for 1in (2–3cm) **(F)**.

Step 2: Pull the yarn through.

Step 3: Rotate the work then thread the needle back through the same stitches **(G)**, skipping the first stitch. Pull the yarn tight and trim it close to the work.

BLOCKING

Blocking describes the method of stretching slightly, and shaping a finished piece of knitting or crochet work, using some form of water. It gives your work a much neater and more professional finish because it relaxes the fibers and evens out your stitches.

Follow the steps to block your granny squares or motifs. You will need blocking boards (usually small boards made of foam that are interlocking to form larger boards), rust-proof glass-headed pins, and a spray water bottle.

Step 1: Using rust-proof glass-headed pins or blocking pins, pin out your motif, with right side uppermost, onto your blocking board to the dimensions specified in your pattern. Gently ease the fabric to the measurements provided, making sure that you do not distort the stitches. Make sure edges are straight or curved, as required **(H)**.

Step 2: Spray your work with cold water until it is damp but not completely saturated.

Step 3: Leave to dry completely then remove the pins.

NOTE: *Spray starch is recommended if you would like to stiffen your pieces (for example with bunting appliqué). Block as usual. When the piece is completely dry, turn over so that the wrong side is uppermost, pin out and spray with spray starch. Leave to dry completely.*

MAKING A TASSEL

Step 1: Take a piece of strong card that is approximately 3in (8cm) long. Wrap yarn around the card approximately 25 times, then cut off the remaining yarn. Thread a short length of the same yarn into a yarn needle and thread it underneath the wrapped yarn at one end. This is the top of the tassel **(I)**.

Step 2: Tie a knot tightly around the wrapped yarn and do not trim these two ends of yarn as you will use them to attach the tassel to the flag. Gently cut the yarn wraps at the bottom of the card **(J)**.

Step 3: Tie another short length of same yarn around the tassel, approximately ½in (1cm) down from the top knot, to create a bulb shape **(K)**. Finally, trim the edge of the tassel straight.

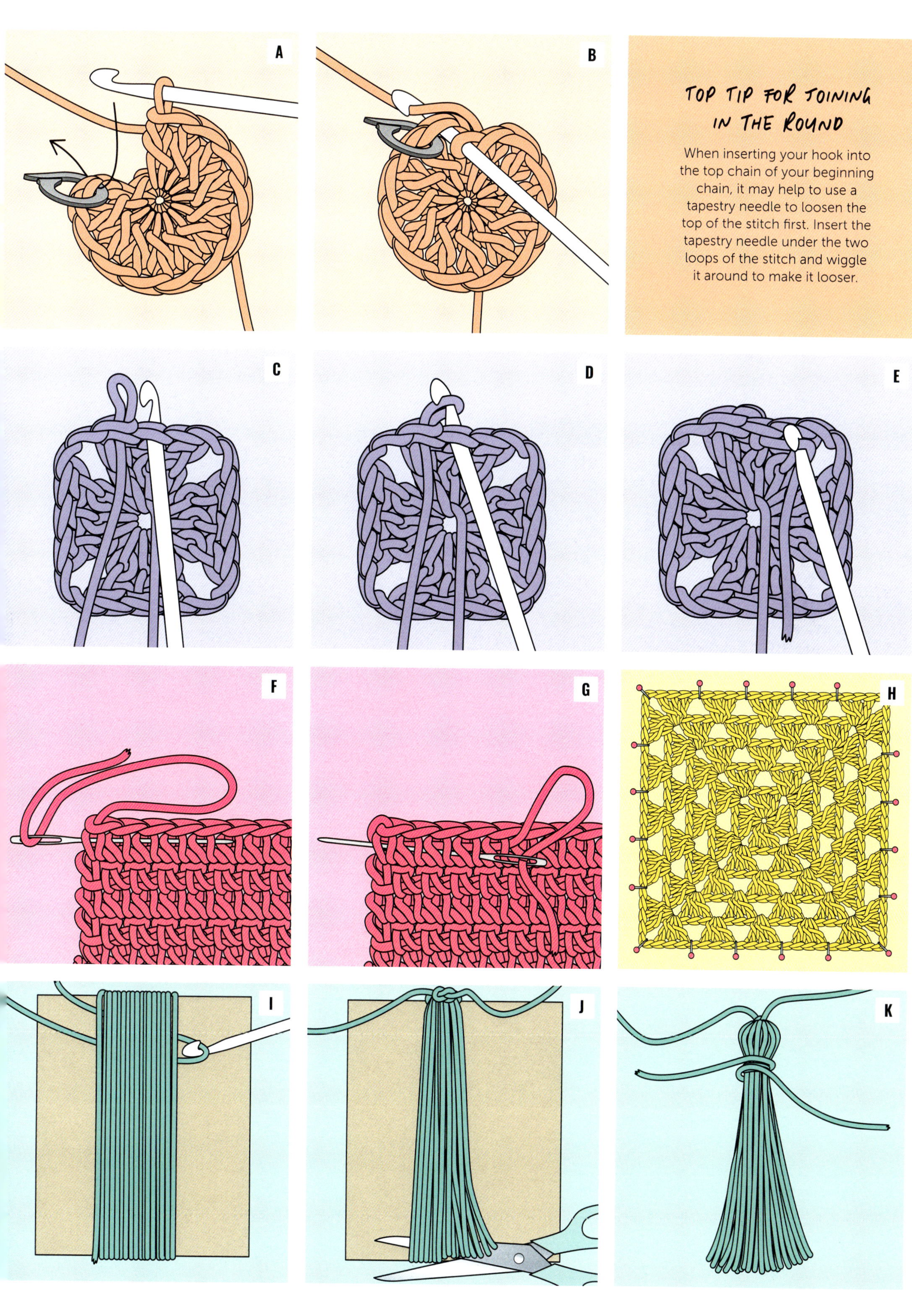
A
B
TOP TIP FOR JOINING IN THE ROUND
When inserting your hook into the top chain of your beginning chain, it may help to use a tapestry needle to loosen the top of the stitch first. Insert the tapestry needle under the two loops of the stitch and wiggle it around to make it looser.
C
D
E
F
G
H
I
J
K

ABOUT THE AUTHOR

Lynne has worked in the heart of the knitting and crochet sector for over 14 years and is passionate about helping others enjoy the wellbeing and creative benefits that both crochet and knitting can bring.

She left her prominent environmental career of 20 years to turn her hobby into her business and hasn't looked back since. After venturing into the world of crochet and knitting, she is now an established designer, editor, and author and has written nine popular craft books including bestseller *The Sock Knitting Bible*. Lynne both edits and features in many of the UK's knitting and crochet magazines with her new designs and informative articles and she is seen as an expert in her field.

By sharing her tips and knowledge, Lynne aims to help crocheters and knitters worldwide to enjoy the calm and relaxing process of turning beautiful yarns into colorful creations, and to improve their confidence by learning new skills.

When Lynne isn't working, you can either find her enjoying the outdoors on local walks or simply relaxing at home with her knitting and crochet, trying not to lose count or drop a stitch.

You can follow her knitting and crochet adventures on her website, where she shares lots of free patterns, tips and advice, or follow her inspiring accounts on social media.

www.knitcrochetcreate.com

Instagram: @the_woolnest

THANKS

I love to share my crochet skills and knowledge, so it was such an honor to research and write this book all about granny squares, one of my favorite things to crochet.

It was a huge task to undertake, and I couldn't have done it without the expert support of my book editor Marie and the wonderful team at David and Charles.

Enormous thanks to Scheepjes for kindly sending me the biggest box of gorgeous yarn for crocheting up samples and making it a joyous task to choose color combinations.

Finally, I have my husband Alex to thank for putting up with my never-ending crochet exploits, and those yarn deliveries that seem to occupy every nook and cranny of the house. His patience knows no bounds, and he provides the best IT support. I couldn't have written this book without him.

And last but not at all least, a huge thank you to everyone who has followed my design journey, or bought one of my books, or attended one of my classes; your continued support is very much appreciated and I'm truly grateful.

Lynne x

SUPPLIERS

Scheepjes, Mercuriusweg 16, 9482 WL Tynaarlo, The Netherlands.

www.scheepjes.com

INDEX

A DAVID AND CHARLES BOOK

David and Charles is an imprint of David and Charles, Ltd
Suite A, Tourism House, Pynes Hill, Exeter, EX2 5WS

First published in the UK and USA in 2025

A catalogue record for this book is available from the British Library.

ISBN-13: 9781446314050 paperback
ISBN-13: 9781446314067 EPUB

This book has been printed on paper from approved suppliers and made from pulp from sustainable sources.

Printed in Turkey through Omur Printing & Packaging for:
David and Charles, Ltd
Suite A, Tourism House, Pynes Hill, Exeter, EX2 5WS

10 9 8 7 6 5 4 3

Publishing Director: Ame Verso
Senior Commissioning Editor: Sarah Callard
Publishing Manager: Jeni Chown
Editor: Victoria Allen
Project Editor: Marie Clayton
Lead Designer: Sam Staddon
Designer: Anna Wade
Pre-press Designer: Susan Reansbury
Illustrations: Kuo Kang Chen
Art Direction: Sarah Rowntree
Photography: Jason Jenkins
Production Manager: Beverley Richardson

Layout of the digital edition of this book may vary depending on reader hardware and display settings.